FAMILY BY GOD'S DESIGN

· ·

A Celebrating Community of Honor and Grace

JOHN SALMON, PHD

WestBow
PRESS
A DIVISION OF THOMAS NELSON

WestBow Press books may be ordered through booksellers or by contacting:

WestBow Press
A Division of Thomas Nelson
1663 Liberty Drive
Bloomington, IN 47403
www.westbowpress.com
1-(866) 928-1240

ISBN: 978-1-4497-1981-4 (sc)
ISBN: 978-1-4497-1983-8 (hc)
ISBN: 978-1-4497-1982-1 (e)

Library of Congress Control Number: 2011932769

Printed in the United States of America

WestBow Press rev. date: 07/18/2011

To my father who honored our family enough to change our generational trajectory. Without his efforts, our family (and my life) would be in a very different place today.

To my mother, the picture of sacrificial grace. I watched her respond with grace to everyone she met.

Together, they taught us how to celebrate and laugh.

Thank you!

CONTENTS

· ·

ACKNOWLEDGMENTS

· ·

Several people have contributed to the completion of this writing project. First, I need to thank Tim Green. Tim, a friend who also facilitates a men's Bible Study I attend, graciously offered to read this manuscript as I wrote it. He offered wonderful suggestions and insights that helped me "think through" various concepts and how to best communicate those ideas to the reader. Tim is a true family man who makes intentional effort to shape his family after God's design. He heads a household that truly is a celebrating community of honor and grace.

I also thank Terry Lutz, a college roommate and dear friend. Terry read the manuscript as I prepared it and discussed various ideas with me. He has offered much appreciated encouragement and support throughout our friendship.

In seeking an editor to review my work I had the good fortune to discover Scott Philip Stewart,, PhD, at Christian Author Services. Dr. Stewart was able to review my manuscript and maintain the intent of the concepts while adding depth and clarity to their expression. I thoroughly enjoyed working with him.

As noted in the dedication, I have to thank my mother and father. They modeled many of the concepts throughout this book. As I grow older and watch my own children learn and grow, I have come to better appreciate the role my parents have played in my life. I have come to realize how fortunate I am to have grown up in a Christian home that looked to God for the design of life.

Finally, I must thank my wife and children. My daughters have proven very patient while I wrote this book. They have graciously allowed me to share stories about them to make various points. Although my daughters are only in their teen years, they are lovely young women. I love watching them mature and find myself learning so much about life and God through their wisdom and insights. They have made me rich, not in finances but in relationship.

I have a truly gracious and loving wife, Alicia. She not only supports me but brings out the best in me. She has become the Michelangelo to my slab of clay. Alicia deserves more gratitude and love than I can express. She is an amazing woman and wonderful mother as well. I am very thankful that she is my wife in this journey of family. Alicia deserves the lion's share of credit for helping to make our family a respite from the world, a place of celebration. In Alicia I have found a "good thing" and "obtained favor from the LORD" (Proverbs 18:22-NASB).

INTRODUCTION:
CHANGING TIMES AND ORIGINAL DESIGNS

In his book *The Intentional Family: How to Build Family Ties in Our Modern World,* William Doherty (1997) presents an interesting history of the family. He states that prior to the 1920s, family was structured around community ties, kinship, and the family unit. Extended family members often lived close to one another and remained involved in one another's lives. Children provided economic support to the family by contributing to the family business or by supporting the family through work outside the family. The family's primary goal was to provide family members with stability and security. Individual happiness remained secondary.

My great aunt exemplifies this *community* model of family. As the oldest daughter in her family, she quit high school so she could go to work and help provide financial support for the family. Her income enabled her younger sisters to complete high school and even attend post-high school training. She sacrificed her personal achievement to provide for her family's stability.

Between the 1920s and 1950s what many of us think of as the *traditional family* replaced the *community family* as the primary model. In this family model a stable married couple with close emotional bonds, good communication, and apparent partnership in childrearing stood at the head of the traditional family. The emergence of the traditional family initiated a slight shift in the primary goal of the family. The personal achievement and happiness of each individual family member grew more important. Whereas in the *community family* the individual's role was to promote the well-being of the family, in the *traditional family* the family's role was to promote the happiness and achievement of the individual. Thus, the emphasis shifted from *one-for-all* to *all-for-one*. The balance between individual happiness and family stability shifted toward individual happiness.

Beginning in the 1960s and 1970s, the priority of the individual continued to grow, and over the next several decades the family continued to change. The primary goal of each individual became finding personal happiness. Family stability and security became secondary to personal happiness. If marriage did not bring a spouse personal happiness, he or she could leave the marriage. The incidence of divorce increased from about 20% in 1960 to nearly 45% in 2000 (Witherspoon, 2006). The number of single parents increased as more people divorced or bore children out of wedlock. Remarriage resulted in a growing number of "blended families." TV shows such as *The Brady Bunch* began to reflect—and even romanticize—this change. People began to create, or find themselves in, various family configurations. No single configuration was considered inherently better than any other. We became, in William Doherty's estimation, the first society in history with no clear social consensus of what constitutes the "best family."

Doherty suggests that families must now make a choice between two options. (1) They can allow society's pull for individual happiness and entitlement to shape their family, or (2) they can *intentionally* create a family with intimate relationships. They can either allow the family to disconnect and drift toward the waterfalls of isolation or they can work together to connect and move up river to greater intimacy and emotional connection. To intentionally create an emotionally intimate family, family members must pull together, put muscle to oar, and work together against the natural drift of society. This demands thoughtful action and intentional effort.

The Natural Drift

Survivor has become one of the top-rated shows on TV. According to Nielsen Media Research, 13.1 million viewers watched the second week of *Survivor: Gabon* as contestants competed to be the "last one standing" (nytimes.com, 10/4/08). Players started the game divided into teams. Each time a team lost, team members voted a member (the "weak link") off the show. Eventually, the remaining players formed one team and continued to vote someone off the show until only one person remained (survived). To survive, individual contestants formed temporary alliances to protect themselves while competing for the ultimate goal of individual success.

Families that do not intentionally work to build relationships find themselves caught in a cultural drift that casts them in their own season of *Survivor*. Like the cast of the show, individual family members form temporary alliances while striving for the goal of *individual* happiness. As the episode progresses, family members assume the power to "vote" those who do not live up to certain ideals, or those who pose a threat to individual happiness, off the family. Although family members may make alliances to reach individual goals, if one member of the alliance does not live up to his "end of the bargain," he is "voted" off the family. Ultimately, each individual is seeking his own self-centered end.

Let's take a short trip downstream, following society's drift, to explore where this *Survivor* mentality has taken the family.

The Falls of Individualism

As we move downstream, we see the family drifting away from a community and family orientation toward an individualistic orientation. The result is that the individual works to achieve personal goals of wealth and happiness rather than the security of other family members. Individual family members form alliances in the pursuit of personal happiness and break those alliances when they do not bring the desired "payoff." Marriage, for instance, has become for many simply an alliance that "partners" enter into to ensure *individual* happiness. When individual happiness proves difficult to achieve within the alliance, the spouse is "voted out" of the alliance and a new alliance is created.

As the stream flows down over the falls of individualism, marriage has become an expendable commodity—especially when one partner does not make the other partner happy. Partners no longer believe it important to enhance one another's lives. Instead, each one expects family to enhance his or her own (individual) life. If family does not enhance the individual's life, the individual may simply break his alliance with the family. For instance, statistics suggest that divorce rates remain at about 45% for all first marriages (Duda, 2003; Witherspoon, 2006). Unfortunately, the divorce rate for Christians is similar to that of non-Christians (Barna, 2008). Furthermore, as many as 37% of married men and 20% of married women report having have had an extramarital affair (Spring, 1996). These statistics show the price of not finding individual satisfaction in a relationship and "voting" the partner out of the family in order to form new alliances.

Near the falls of individualism, parenting is viewed as a service parents provide to children. Children are expected to pay for this service with the currency of love and affection. Children are seen as tools to fulfill a parent's individual purposes, an opportunity to pass on personal ideals and a chance to live out unfulfilled dreams. Under the guise of "giving my child the best opportunities" and "proving myself a good parent, adored by my children," parents push their children beyond their developmental capabilities and natural time-constraints and create a generation of "hurried children" (Elkind, 1981). They rush children from activity to activity and afford them no free time to "just be kids" and recharge. In fact, unstructured time for children between the ages of 3 and 12 years dropped by 50% between 1981 and 1997. Free time has decreased to 12 hours per week during the same time period (Doherty, 1997). Children's lives are rushed and hurried as they try to live up to parental and cultural expectations and make installments to pay off the great debt they "owe" parents for the parental services they receive.

Although children initially accept this alliance and work to please their parents, they never develop a sense of self outside of their parents' demands. When they interfere with parental happiness or show too little gratitude, parents become angry and threaten to "send them away." Parents may say such things as "why does my child always take and never give? I can't wait until he finally leaves and gives me some space." When children do break the alliance by growing up and becoming more independent (as they all do), they are often voted out of the family and ignored, belittled, or isolated.

The Falls of Entitlement

This increased focus on individual happiness and rights also creates a sense entitlement. Each individual feels *entitled* to happiness and personal fulfillment, both of which are considered limited commodities for which we must compete. An immature "gimme mentality" dominates families as they near the falls of entitlement. Children and parents want freedom without responsibility. Family members feel entitled to happiness and entertainment. If family members do not feel the family provides the happiness and entertainment they "deserve," they search for it outside the family in extramarital affairs, work, pornography, alcohol, or obsessive hobbies, among other things. Unfortunately, the family *cannot* make a person happy or keep them entertained. Family does provide a measure of happiness, but it also provides opportunities for growth that entail some stress and strain.

Downstream Without a Paddle

Finally, the increased demand for individual happiness creates a "boot-strapper" mentality. Families become increasingly performance-oriented, operating out of a punishment mentality. We hear statements such as "he made his own bed, now let him lie in it." We lose sight of grace and compassion. We find ourselves downstream without a paddle.

This focus on performance can also lead to legalism within families. Love becomes a commodity to earn. Family members risk losing love unless they live up to individual standards and achieve the "right ends." Love and acceptance are based not on who the person is but on his or her style of dress, appearance, and good deeds. Misbehavior is perceived as a lack of love, and withholding love is a form of discipline. A child's sense of worth becomes tied to what he can do and accomplish rather than who he is as a person. He always feels the need to "live up" to an unreasonable or impossible standard to earn acceptance and love. Family members keep score of good deeds and "brownie points," monitoring one another's standing in the contest to obtain the "last available drop" of attention and love. As a result, children constantly feel unloved, unworthy, and unlovable, burdened and stressed by the constant pressure to perform up to some arbitrary standard. They find themselves careening downstream toward the falls without a raft and without support.

Another aspect of performance orientation is that it may lead to elitism. Family members in the "elite family" shine a judgmental light on other families (Kimmel, 2004). They point out other families' flaws and mistakes. They look down on other families that are different. Moreover, such families adopt a "holier-than-thou" attitude and refuse to associate with those whom they judge as "less" well-dressed, talented, or spiritual. In pointing out the flaws of other people they elevate themselves to an elite position.

The Bottom of the Falls

Families continue the drift toward disengagement and disconnection as each individual feels increasingly entitled to seek his or her own individual goals at the expense of others. Eventually, family members plunge over the falls and find themselves in turbulent waters, sucked under by the strong currents of society. Isolation trumps community and togetherness. Each family member listens to music through IPods and earphones, never sharing enjoyable moments or discoveries with other family members. While traveling as a family, each child watches his movie of choice on his own individual DVD player, while up front each adult listens to individually chosen music. All wear earphones, making it impossible to share or hear any input from others in the car. At home, busy schedules preclude family time. Children are rushed from one activity to another while parents try to squeeze in a Big Mac and a workout between the shuffling of kids.

Even in our churches we separate families, sending children to worship services designed specifically for their age group, men to men's classes, and women to women's classes. I'm not disparaging classes designed for specific demographics. But we, as a church, may need to rethink our value of the importance of family rather than simply flowing with the cultural drift of treating families as a collection of individuals.

The River's Source

Let's turn our boat around and row upstream, against the natural drift, to discover the alternative family lifestyle of the intentional Christian family. To do so, we must travel all the way upstream to discover the beginning of the stream, the source of the intentional Christian family.

God designed the family and gave it a central role in His plan. His plan began when He created the family on the sixth day of creation, and His plan will end with the ultimate wedding reception of the Bridegroom, Jesus Christ, to His Bride, the Church. From Adam and Eve to the great wedding feast of Heaven, God designed the family to mirror His image in a fallen world. Each aspect of the family offers a clear reflection of the image of God.

Reflections of God in the Pool of Marriage

God exists in the relationship of "Three in One." When a man marries a woman, they become one flesh. A man leaves his mother and father in order to "cleave" to his wife (Genesis 2:22-25). Two become one, reflecting the three-in-one relationship of the God-head. Mysteriously, God the Father, God the Son, and God the Holy Spirit are unique individuals with distinct roles yet are a unity, completely one. As a reflection of this mystery, a man and a woman marry to become completely one yet maintain their unique individuality and the distinct roles of husband and wife.

Jesus, our Loving Husband, sacrificed His own desires for the good of His bride, the Church. He seeks to lift her and glorify her. In the pool of marriage, husbands love their wives in a similar manner, reflecting God's relational unity and Christ's relationship to the church (Ephesians 5:25-30).

Jesus submitted to His Father, obediently following God's plan to redeem mankind. Although our contemporary culture fights against submission, Christ embraced it and humbly submitted (Philippians 2:5-9) and entrusted Himself to God (1 Peter 2:21-3:2). In Christ, we see the perfect picture of submission to a loving God. In a Christian marriage, each member is called to submit to one another (Ephesians 5:21-22), reflecting Christ's submission to God.

Reflections of God in the Parent-Child Relationship

Scripture presents many examples of God as Parent. For instance, God is our Father and we are His adopted children. We come to Him saying, "Abba" Daddy (Romans 8:15). God also compares Himself to a nursing mother, adoring and comforting her children (Isaiah 66:12-13). In both cases, we are His children, brothers of Christ, and joint-heirs with Jesus Christ (Romans 8:17). Children adoringly approach their father, calling him Daddy and trusting him to provide their needs. This reflects our adoption as children of God.

Parent-child relationships in a godly family will mirror God's Fatherhood and our adoption into His family.

The River's True Source

As we finally move to the true source of the family, we find God Himself. God designed the family to reflect His glory and draw people to Him. Is it any wonder that Satan has waged an all-out attack on the family? He certainly rejoices in broken marriages and broken homes. The more he can destroy the family, the more people he can tear away from God.

We need to reclaim the family for God. That reclamation must begin in the church. If we simply allow our families to be pulled into the cultural drift of self-focus and the resulting disconnection, we will lose the battle for our families and our children. The intentional Christian family moves upstream toward the True Source of the family. The intentional Christian family works to move toward the True Source and, in so doing, becomes a celebrating community of honor and grace.

A celebrating community of honor and grace.... This definition has three characteristics of the intentional Christian family: honor, grace, and celebrating community. These three qualities separate the intentional Christian family from the world and the prevailing culture and reclaim the family for Christ.

A Celebrating Community of Honor and Grace

This book focuses on the intentional Christian family as a celebrating community of honor and grace. The first section will explore the intentional Christian family as *a place of honor, reflecting the image of God*. Family members "give preference to one another in honor" (Romans 12:10). Each family member humbly gives the needs and interests of other family members priority equal to or above his own. The members honor one another by valuing and cherishing each other, submitting to one another's requests, and learning of one another's interests. Intentional Christian families show honor by recognizing each family member's strengths and giving thanks to one another.

The second section will focus on the intentional Christian family as *a place of grace*, a place where family members give generously to one another with no expectations of repayment. Instead of giving with a "tit for tat" attitude, members of the intentional Christian family give one another the best of their time, effort, and forgiveness with no strings attached. Gracious family members not only forgive each other's offenses but repay insult with blessing. They speak to one another with grace-filled words.

The third section will focus on the intentional Christian family as *a celebrating community*. More than any other group of people, Christians have reason to celebrate. Honor and grace lay the foundation for the intimate fellowship of celebration. Routines and rituals emphasize the priorities of honoring one another and growing in relation to one another.

So hop in the boat, grab an oar, and join me upstream to explore the family by God's design: a celebrating community of honor and grace.

DIAMONDS OR COAL

. . . .

"Marriage requires a radical commitment to love our spouses as they are, while longing for them to become what they are not yet. Every marriage moves either toward enhancing one another's glory or toward degrading each other."

Dan Allender and Tremper Longman III

"If you treat a man as he is, he will stay as he is. But if you treat him as if he were what he ought to be and could be, he will become the bigger and better man."

Johann Wolfgang von Goethe

Diamonds or Coal

Imagine a lump of coal and a diamond ring. Both are composed of carbon and both serve a unique purpose. If a chunk of coal remains buried under 435,113 pounds of pressure per square inch and remains at temperatures of about 752 degrees Fahrenheit, its carbon composition purifies and its structure modifies to form a different kind of carbon. After this purer form of carbon is mined, a jeweler places it in quick drying cement and cuts a groove in it. He inserts a steel blade into that groove and hits it to cut the carbon into pieces. The jeweler then removes the cut pieces of carbon from the cement and places them in a lathe. Working with another piece of diamond as a cutting tool, the jeweler cuts the pieces into the more familiar shape of a diamond (http://howstuffworks.com/diamond.htm). So goes the journey of carbon from coal to diamond. In this sense, you may think of a lump of coal as a diamond in the rough.

Interestingly, diamonds are no more rare than other gems (http://howstuffworks.com/diamond4.htm), which raises a question. If diamonds and coal are both carbons and they are not more rare than other gems, why do we value diamonds so much more? According to howstuffworks. com, we value diamonds more than other gems because of marketing and ownership. Perhaps, the right marketer could buy his beloved fiancé a lump of coal instead of a diamond ring and convince her of its value. Wouldn't the ladies just love that?

Even knowing all this, however, if I offer you a bag of diamonds or a bag of coal, which would you take? I could try to convince you of coal's value by saying it can help keep you warm and help cook your food; but, you would most likely pay more for a single diamond than for several bins of coal.

Let's face it, we have learned to value diamonds more than coal. We treat diamonds with more respect and care. We continue to honor our fiancés with diamond rings rather than bags of coal. We honor diamonds by treating them with care and respect while we throw coal in the furnace by the shovelful for our own comfort. We honor diamonds by giving them value and treating them as precious while we toss coal aside to trample under foot or on the fire to warm up a burger.

Do you treat the members of your family like diamonds or coal? Do you treat them with care and respect, or do you throw them in the fire to use for your comfort? Do you honor them by giving them value and treating them as precious or dishonor them by tossing them aside to trample under foot?

Honor is one of the defining characteristics of the intentional Christian family. In order to show honor, members of an intentional Christian family treat one another with care and respect. They value one another as precious and treat one another as special. They learn to honor one another as diamonds among coal.

Our Example

God set the perfect example for how we are to honor others. He honored us by making us the crown of His creation, the very image of God (Genesis 1, Psalm 8). Even more, He honored us by taking on the form of a man when He came to earth in the person of Jesus Christ. He honored us so much that He humbly became a man and shared our humanity (Philippians 2:5-11).

Just as God honors us, we are to honor one another. We treat one another as valuable and worthy of respect because God created us in His image. We are "fearfully and wonderfully made" (Psalm 139:14), a little lower than the angels (Psalm 8), and God's masterpiece (Ephesians 2:10). A person has great value because he is a creation of God, created in the very image of God.

A Christian's Call to Honor

God calls the Christian to honor all men (Romans 12:10). More specifically, He calls us to honor members of our family. Scripture tells us to hold marriage in honor (Hebrews 13:4). A Christian husband honors his wife, praising her among the people (Proverbs 31:28-29). He honors her with sacrificial love (Ephesians 5: 25-30), placing her needs above his own interests. The extent to which a man honors (values) his wife even influences the effectiveness of his prayer life (1 Peter 3:7).

A Christian wife is also called to honor her husband. As the "crown of her husband" (Proverbs 12:4), her work adds to his name and value among the other men (Proverb 31:21). She honors him by increasing his value and submitting to his authority in Christ (Ephesians 5:21-22).

Moreover, Christian parents honor their children, recognizing them as a gift from God (Psalm 127:3-5). They realize the responsibility of honoring their children's purpose in God by guiding them to their target as marksmen aim their arrow for the bulls-eye (Psalm 127:4). They honor their children's God-given personality and abilities by encouraging and guiding the use of those gifts (Proverbs 22:6). To do this, parents honor their children by remaining available to them—available to encourage, guide, and love. Parents also honor their children by affirming them, communicating their value and worth in words and deeds. Parents also honor their children in holding their children accountable to a godly lifestyle.

God also commands children to honor their parents (Ephesians 6:1). In fact, the command to honor one's parents is "the first commandment with a promise," the promise of long life (Ephesians 6:1), peace (Proverbs 3:1-2), and understanding (Proverbs 4:1).

As a family practices honor in all these relationships, siblings will learn to honor each other as well. Though at times they will still argue and disagree, they will learn that honor is a priority in the family and that each family member owes honor and deserves honor from all other family members.

The Result of Honor

Honoring people liberates them to live out the potential God has given them. Perhaps you've heard the story* of the "14-cow woman." The story tells of a missionary who lived on a Pacific island. During his stay, natives told him about a man from a neighboring island who had given 14-cows as a dowry for one of the island women. The islanders laughed because this man had paid so high a price for such an ugly, clumsy, lazy woman. They were glad to get rid of her and amazed to have won such a high dowry for her. The missionary's curiosity about this woman increased until he decided to go to the neighboring island and meet the man who paid such a high dowry for a woman of so little value.

One day he took his boat to the neighboring island to meet this man. A woman met him as he landed his boat. She helped him pull his boat onto the shore and listened as he explained who he wanted to see. The woman volunteered to accompany him to the man's house. As they walked, he began to admire the woman's grace and beauty. He wondered why a man from this island would go to a neighboring island to find a wife when such a beautiful woman lived on his own island.

When they finally arrived at the man's home, the woman offered the missionary a seat on the patio and disappeared. A moment later the woman returned with the man. She introduced him to the missionary and, as they began talking, she brought drinks and refreshments. Then she sat down and joined in the conversation, asking about the missionary, his work, and his journeys. After a short time, she excused herself explaining that she had several more tasks to complete before the afternoon was over.

The man followed her with his eyes. He smiled and began to tell the missionary about this wonderful woman: loving, gracious, intelligent, and beautiful. He obviously adored her. The missionary, although he understood the man's adoration for this woman, was confused. He asked, "Why would you pay 14 cows for another woman when you obviously adore this woman so much?"

The man burst into laughter. "She is the woman for whom I paid 14 cows... and worth twice that! The men of her island have no idea how amazing and valuable this woman is!"

The missionary was stunned. How could the natives have thought of this woman as ugly, clumsy, and lazy? Finally, he explained his confusion.

The man smiled thoughtfully and then explained. "The people of her home island did not honor her, so she did not honor herself. She lived to their level of dishonor. I honored her; I willingly gave a high price for her and, in so doing, showed her great honor. With such honor bestowed upon her, her view of herself began to change. As she lived in the gratitude of the honor received, she changed. She became more caring, more generous, more confident...and more willing to love the one who honors her. As we receive honor, we grow into our greatest potential; and, in this case, I get the fringe benefit of a wife with great beauty...both inside and out."

(*I cannot recall where I heard the story of the "14-cow woman." I read a very similar rendition of this story, however, in *Kosher Sex* by Rabbi ShmuleyBoteach.)

The story of the 14-cow woman may sound somewhat farfetched, but consider the Song of Solomon. In the first chapter we find a young woman asking her lover not to look at her because she is "swarthy, for the sun has burned me…I have not taken care of my own vineyards" (1:6). She expresses self-doubt and self-deprecation. She does not consider herself lovely. Her lover honors her, however, by calling her the "most beautiful among women" (1:8, 15) and a "lily among thorns" (2:2). In response to this honor, the bride finds confidence in herself. She begins to see her own beauty and calls herself the "rose of Sharon," the "lily of the valleys" (2:1). His honor lifted her and brought her confidence. She became a stronger and more dedicated bride. In response to the great honor her lover bestowed on her she grew into the Masterpiece that God had created (Ephesians 2:10).

An older gentleman once told me about his wife who had died several months prior to our conversation. He shared how much he missed her. He recalled her beauty and joy, graciousness and kindness. He spoke fondly of her love, her cooking, and her conversation. Finally he looked at me with tears in his eyes and said, "She made me the person I am today. I am a better person because of her. She taught me to love." She had honored him as her husband and he had become a better man because of that honor.

When we honor someone we place value on them and, in words and actions, we express that value to them. As a result, the person begins to internalize the value we give them. The person changes to match the honor and value we give. Give little honor and the person responds a little. Give great honor and the person will grow to live a life worthy of such great honor.

The Danger of Dishonor

Honor changes people. Dishonor does, too. Family therapists such as Bert Hellinger (1998) and Murray Bowen (Scalise, 2008) describe how dishonor impacts the family. Those who dishonor family members are often left with unresolved bitterness, anger, and shame that binds them to the person they dishonor. The bitterness, anger, and shame affect the person's behavior and mood. Unfortunately, this person may pass his unresolved "emotional baggage" onto the next generation as the pent-up anger and shame explode unexpectedly into current family relationships. A comment or facial expression can trigger a cascade of anger or shame from the person who dishonors another family member. As this happens, the dishonor creates an environment that perpetuates dishonor and strains relationships to the point that one person in the family may actually repeat the dishonored person's behavior. Consider this example.

Jack came to my office because his teenage daughter was "driving him crazy." She was "acting like her grandfather." As I explored Jack's relationship with his father, Jack noted that he and his father had a good relationship all through childhood. He had felt loved and cared for. As he moved into adolescence, however, things began to change. As Jack spent more time with his friends and made more decisions on his own, his father became more demanding and expressed his disapproval in harsher ways. Their relationship became strained, filled with disagreements, loud arguments, name calling, and bitter words. Jack eventually left home angry at his father and bitter about the arguments that had filled his adolescent years.

Jack's anger *seemed* to disappear since he was away from his father, but inside he remained bitter and resentful. When others asked him about his father, he would mention his father's mistakes and shortcomings. As time passed, Jack fell in love, got married, and had children. All went well until his daughter reached adolescence. He saw her becoming more like his father, arguing with him and making unrealistic demands. What disturbed him more was his own reaction. He found himself angry, making unrealistic demands, and harshly criticizing her decisions. Though he knew he was wrong and did not want to engage in this behavior, he simply did not know how to stop.

As we talked, he realized that his daughter's adolescent behavior made him feel just as he had felt during his own adolescence. He recognized some of his father's actions in her and lashed out at her with held-over anger at his father. He began to realize that he had dishonored his father since adolescence. He had focused so much on what he disliked about his father that he had forgotten what he liked. He had allowed that anger to grow and bind him to a part of his father that did not represent the love they had shared. This anger bubbled to the surface and exploded when his daughter reached adolescence. His dishonor toward his father created an environment of dishonor that eventually led to a strained relationship with his daughter.

The Bible suggests this principle as well. Recall how, after the flood, Noah got drunk and passed out in his tent...naked (Genesis 5:20-29). His shame was open for all to see. One of his sons, Ham, saw him passed out naked. He did not value his father enough to cover his nakedness. Instead, he left his father in this dishonorable state. He further dishonored his father by telling his brothers about their father's shame. He undermined his father's authority by publishing his sin.

On the other hand, his brothers honored their father by looking away as they covered him. They honored him enough to hide this image of shame from their eyes. They did not broadcast their father's sin to other people. Instead, they protected their father's honor.

Because Ham dishonored his father, his descendants were cursed to become the servants of his brothers' descendants. He had passed down a curse of dishonor to his descendants, especially through his son Canaan (Genesis 9:20-27).

God calls us to honor one another. His word, the Bible, reveals the blessings of honor and the dangers of dishonor. Honored people live out the honor they receive. Honoring others helps to create an environment that encourages love and more honor. Dishonor, on the other hand, leads to curses. Anger, bitterness, and resentment grow from dishonor and create an environment that perpetuates more dishonor, cursing family members to lives of sorrow, pain, and strained relationships.

Becoming a Person of Honor

To create a family of honor, we must obey God's call to honor. We must also strive to become a person worthy of honor. What makes a person worthy of honor? Solomon, the wisest man of his time, helps us answer that question by presenting several characteristics of a person worthy of honor.

First, Solomon tells us that *a gracious person attains honor* (Proverbs 11:16). Grace is another attribute of the intentional Christian family that we will explore in the next section. For now, though, it is important to recognize that a person of grace—a gracious person—attains honor.

Second, Solomon notes that *a person worthy of honor is humble* (Proverbs 15:33). In fact, humility is the flip side of honor. Paul tells us to "do nothing from selfishness or empty conceit, but with humility of mind let each of you regard one another as more important than himself; do not look out for your own personal interests, but also the interests of others" (Philippians 2:3-4). In other words, humbly honor one another. A humble person honors other people and is worthy of honor.

No one wants to be around a person full of pride and arrogance. We grow bored listening to an arrogant person talk about his accomplishments to the neglect of anyone else's achievements. But we all admire a humble person. We value time spent with a person who humbly attends to us during our time together. We love to be with a person who humbly honors us. We naturally honor a humble person.

A humble person does several things that make him a person worthy of honor. He listens to and accepts discipline, which leads to honor (Proverbs 13:18). We all make mistakes and do wrong things due to inexperience, hurry, or ignorance. A humble person, however, is willing to accept advice from others. He believes that others have important contributions to make and, as a result, he takes those contributions to heart. He realizes that the contributions of others do not in any way minimize his own efforts.

A humble person also avoids quarrels and strife whenever possible. He loves peace and avoids unnecessary arguments. He remains accepting of other people in spite of differences of opinion. Wouldn't you agree that such a person is worthy of honor (Proverbs 20:3)?

Setting the Tone

Parents play a huge role in setting the tone of honor in a home. When parents behave in away that promotes honor, they set the stage for the whole family to honor one another. When parents behave dishonorably towards each other or other members of the family (their parents, their siblings, their children), on the other hand, they set the stage for trouble. Jesus told his disciples that "stumbling blocks" are inevitable, but "woe to that man through whom the stumbling block comes!" He also said, "Whoever causes one of these little ones who believe in Me to stumble, it is better for him to have a heavy millstone hung around his neck, and to be drowned in the depths of the sea" (Matthew 18:6-7). Perhaps this could be said of one who makes his child or spouse stumble by living a dishonorable life.

Noah acted dishonorably by getting drunk, and his drunken state set the stage for his son Ham to stumble. Indirectly, Noah's dishonorable behavior led to the cursing of his own grandchildren. What a terrible price to pay for a moment of dishonor!

I don't know about you, but my own example as a father and husband is not always one of honor, even though I strive to practice honor daily. We all struggle to honor our family on a consistent basis. Perhaps we can ask ourselves some hard questions to help us continue to act honorably within our families:

- Does my spouse experience me as gracious? Do I set an example of grace for my children? Do I respond with grace when cut off in traffic? Am I unnecessarily harsh toward my children? Do I forgive an offense or hold a grudge?

- Could my spouse readily give examples of my humility? Do I set an example of humility or of self-centeredness for my children? Do I admit when I am wrong? Can no one talk to me when my favorite show or sporting event comes on TV? Does my work take precedence over my family? Do I only allow my music in the car?

- Do my spouse and children experience me as teachable? Or, do I disregard input from my family members and adopt a "my way or the highway" approach, no matter what?

We could ask more questions, but you get the point. If we act in a dishonorable manner, we set the stage for our children to stumble into the sin of dishonoring their parents and then watching them suffer the consequences of dishonor in their lives. We, as parents and spouses, must become people of honor and establish a tradition of honor for our families—for our own generation and those to come.

Members of an intentional Christian family choose to honor and to live honorably. We seek to honor those within our family and strive to become a person worthy of our family's honor. In response to God's command, we choose to honor the members of our family *whether they deserve it or not* and we strive to live a life worthy of receiving honor from the other members of our family. Both honoring others and living honorably are necessary components of the intentional Christian family.

Sacred Moments

When we honor other family members, we place a high value on them. We respect and esteem them. We believe they have good intentions in spite of failures and mistakes. We accept them in spite of disagreements or arguments and continue to believe in and affirm their value and positive intent. We believe they have the wisdom to learn from their failures and mistakes without our harsh judgment and condemnation.

Honor not expressed is no honor at all. Honor demands action. With this in mind, we behave toward family members in such a way that they feel valued and respected. We give them our time, our energy, and our affection. We honor them as a diamond among coal.

Family members feel valued when we treat them as special. They feel honored when we place their interests at a level equal to or above our own and when we accept their point of view as equally valid as our own (or even more so). These moments of honor can be as simple as giving up our desire to watch a particular TV show in order to play a game that another family member wants to play or when we offer a family member the last cookie rather than eat it ourselves.

Every single time we honor a family member we turn a common moment into a sacred moment. The ordinary becomes extraordinary, the mundane, holy. The simple becomes blessed. Indeed, moments of honor become sacred moments that reveal Christ and promote intimacy within a family.

Let's turn our attention to specific ways in which we can encourage sacred moments of honor within our families.

2 KNOWING THE ONES WE HONOR: 101

....

"From knowledge springs not only love but the fortitude to weather marital [and family] storms. Couples [and families] who have detailed love maps of each other's worlds are far better prepared to cope with stressful events and conflicts."

—John Gottman, *The Seven Principles for Making Marriage Work*

Alicia did not know how to honor her family and now she sat in my office crying. Her 9-year-old daughter and 4-year-old son had lived with her sister for the previous 4 years. They did not seem the least bit interested in her. In fact, the 9-year-old was quite angry and wanted Alicia to leave them alone. Alicia explained that she and her children had lived together until her husband, and their father, died. Unfortunately, she admitted that she had not honored them during that time, even when her husband was living. Instead, she had left her children in the house with no supervision while she went out with friends, leaving her daughter (then 5-years-old) to fix her infant brother's breakfast and change his dirty diapers. After her husband died, she had followed various boyfriends from place to place, chasing various "money-making schemes." All the while, her children had little stability and she took no time to learn about their development or interests. Things thus went from bad to worse.

Alicia's family eventually stepped in. They agreed that Alicia's sister and her sister's husband would keep the children while Alicia "got her life together." While her children were living with their aunt and uncle, Alicia made minimal attempts to contact them. She did not send cards on birthdays or holidays and only called occasionally. The children adjusted well to living with their aunt and uncle. Over a 4-year period, they established a strong family bond with their aunt and uncle. The aunt and uncle honored the children by learning about them and supporting their unique interests, talents, and strengths. As a result, the children felt secure with their aunt and uncle.

After all this time Alicia began missing her children and decided that she wanted to have a relationship them. She moved into a home in their neighborhood and began scheduling visits with them. Her work schedule and various recreational activities took priority over her children, however. If the scheduled visitation time conflicted with her other activities, she would forfeit the visits with her children. Even worse, she did not even bother to call to let the aunt and uncle know she could not make it. So the children would be ready and waiting at the arranged time only to grow increasingly frustrated each time she did not show up. When she did visit, she dishonored the aunt and uncle with false accusations about them in front of the children. These accusations upset the children who had learned to love and trust their aunt and uncle. She further dishonored her children by forcing them to participate in activities of interest to *her* while neglecting activities that the children enjoyed.

When she came to see me, she had been living near her children for a little over a year. I began to ask her about her children. "What do they like to eat?" "What do they do for fun?" "What kind of activities are they involved in?" She didn't know. She had no idea what foods her children liked to eat, what activities they enjoyed, the friends they played with, or the hobbies they enjoyed. If I asked about her own hobbies, however, such as organic foods, she could talk for hours. If I brought up the subject of exercise, she could recite rigorous, detailed training regimens. But she could not tell me one thing about her children.

Further discussion revealed that Alicia did not know what to expect from her children or how to talk with children that age. She did not have an age-appropriate expectation for what her children could do or how her children could manage emotions and relationships. We had to face a hard truth. She had no mental model of her children's lives. Her lack of involvement with, and the resulting lack of knowledge about, her children revealed a lack of honor for her children.

The truth is, we make time to learn about those things we love and value. We spend time being with and learning about those things we value. We talk about things we love. If we want to honor members of our family, we need to learn about them. We need to become a student of their life. We need to give attention to the details of their lives and become intimately familiar with their world. This may sound simplistic, but it is foundational to honoring one another.

The Holographic Image

In the movie *Star Wars* characters did not send secret messages in cryptic shorthand, text messages, or e-mail. Instead, they loaded a holographic image of themselves conveying the message into an android. The android would then find the recipient of the message and cast a holographic model of the sender into the middle of the room. The person receiving the message heard the words of the message straight from the receiver's mouth...well, his *holographic* mouth anyway. The receiver could also hear the inflection of the messenger's voice and observe the messenger's facial expression and body language as well. The receiving person got a message that included words, inflection, facial expression, and body language, not just a one-dimensional text message with abbreviations.

When we honor our family members by becoming a student of their person, we develop a model of the whole person. We learn to hold a complete model of that person in our mind—not just a one-dimensional view of what they like to do. Members of our family are much more complex and interesting than that. We honor them by exploring the complexity inherent in their person, by learning about their individual characteristics and unique way of moving about the world, by developing a full "holographic model" of their life and world.

Learning all this information may initially appear overwhelming. Relax, don't worry. You don't have to know it all right now. You have a lifetime to learn about your family members. People are complex, changing, and growing all the time. So don't worry if you don't know something now. Just ask. In fact, the very act of asking someone about what they like or enjoy (and don't) shows interest, honor, and respect. Enjoy the process of learning about them and they will enjoy feeling honored by your interest and the growing intimacy between you.

Honoring Development

In order to have a complete and honoring mental image of our family members, we need to learn a little bit about development. How a person thinks and relates to other people changes with age and developmental stage. Understanding how thinking and social skills develop allows us to honor family members with realistic expectations, respectful communication, and loving guidance. It allows us to honor family members by "meeting them where they are" to form intimate relationships and provide loving structure. Let's explore just two areas of development and learn how an understanding of development can help us honor our family.

How Do They Think?

Thinking changes as a person grows and progresses through the various developmental stages we all go through. An infant thinks differently from an adolescent, who thinks differently from a 45-year-old.

Infancy & Toddlerhood

An infant thinks about and explores the world by putting things in his mouth, rubbing them on his cheek, moving them in front of his eyes, and banging them on something else. As he explores his environment in this manner, he learns that objects are real. We honor this young explorer by providing a safe environment to explore and by encouraging playful exploration, even joining in on the fun. Banging on pots, shaking rattles, and playfully encouraging reaching and grasping honors the infant. This play will also help him associate words with various objects, forming the symbols of language and images to think about the world.

Preschool Years

As he moves through toddlerhood and into the preschool years, he will use those images and words to think about things "in his head" even when they are not present. His thoughts will remain rather literal through the preschool years. I remember having a pretend tea party with my daughters. We used Play-Doh for our snacks and spoke with a "sophisticated" accent as we played. I said, "I love Play-Doh at a party" making the "r" sound "sophisticated" to the best of my ability. My youngest daughter, about 3-years-old at the time, heard that I loved "Play-Doh at the potty." She immediately got up and went to the bathroom to flush Play-Doh down the "potty." She took the words she heard very literally. She did not understand the playful accent or the difference between playful ideas and literal ideas. To her, it was all literal.

Preschool children also tend to think everyone else sees the world as *they* see the world. You can observe this when playing Hide-n-Seek with a child. If they cannot see you, they believe you cannot see them. They hide with their legs sticking out, as a huge "lump" under the covers, or simply by covering their own eyes. They cannot see you and so they assume that you cannot see them. Children begin to realize that other people see the world differently than they do around the age of 4 or 5 years.[1]

Young children also look at only one aspect of a situation. For instance, most preschoolers would rather have a penny than a dime because the penny is "bigger." She does not consider the value, simply the size. My daughters would often ask for a drink of water before bed. Not wanting to give them too much to drink at bedtime, I would pour them a small drink in a short, round glass. They would look at the small amount and ask for more. I would pour the water from the short, round glass into a tall, thin glass. The water now appeared to reach "higher" in the glass. They saw only the height, not the height and width of the volume, and thanked me for the extra water. As they moved into the early years of grade school, they grew beyond these limitations. In fact, most children begin to recognize more than one aspect of a situation (for instance, considering both the height and width of a glass) by 7 years old. Realizing these thought patterns, we can honor our children by adjusting our expectations and loving discipline to match their level of thinking.

Elementary Schoolers

Early elementary school children also begin to have a growing ability to see the world from other viewpoints. Initially, this ability remains concrete, but it continues to expand throughout the elementary school years. As a father, I remember watching with pride as my daughter and her friends played soccer. As a psychologist, I recall watching with great interest as their ability to take another person's perspective emerged as the soccer seasons passed. At 4 or 5 years old, the children all huddled around the ball. They had only one thing on their mind: kick the ball in the goal! Coaches encouraged them to "spread out," but the children still hovered over the ball. As they matured, some of the children slowly began to spread out across the field. By the age of 10 or 11, the children could play positions and pass the ball to one another. They could dribble the ball down the field and see several perspectives. They could assess their own perspective of the goal, their opponent's perspective of them, the goalie's perspective of the ball, and the perspective of their teammate who stood across the field. Realizing a teammate had a clearer shot—a realization achieved by taking that person's perspective of the field and goal—she may choose to pass the ball to him for a shot. We honor this growing ability by adjusting our expectations to match our children's developmental ability and calmly talking about how their behavior might impact others.

Pre-Teens & Middle-Schoolers

If you have a teenager, you have probably experienced the "difficult" middle school child. In fact, pre-teens undergo significant changes. As they enter puberty, their bodies begin to change. Hormones change. Even their brains go through a major change and restructure based on relationships and experience.[2] As a result, your 7th grader may suddenly appear less organized and more scattered than ever before. They may appear more absent-minded than they did in elementary school and even lacking in common sense at times. They may become moody and irritable for no apparent reason.

As their brains grow and change based on relationships and experience, honor becomes crucial! We can provide experiences of honor to help restructure the brain on the basis of love and acceptance, laying the groundwork for security, joy, a positive self-image, and strong respect for others. Or we can provide experiences of dishonor that may restructure the brain on the basis of insecurity and self-preservation, laying the groundwork for mistrust, poor self-image, and constant vigilance.

Teenagers/Adolescents

Teens become experts at looking at the world through someone else's eyes. In fact, they may even become too good at it for their own good. They begin to believe that everyone is looking at them. They tend to see themselves through "someone else's eyes" and notice (and accentuate) every perceived flaw and fear that everyone else sees those same imperfections.

Teens not only look at themselves from another person's view, but they look at the world through various viewpoints as well. They compare and contrast all the ideas and perspectives stored in their heads to develop idealistic theories about life and the world. They also develop the ability to think "faster on their feet." As a result, they become better debaters and especially enjoy "debating" with their parents. While they argue, they can hold your argument and those idealistic theories in their mind at the same time, comparing them while they talk to you. They can also keep their long-term goal in mind and work out scenarios to achieve that goal. All of this can result in a series of frustrating discussions between parent and child. Just remember, they are practicing their developing thinking skills. We honor our teens when we offer them unconditional acceptance combined with the freedom necessary to explore ideas within the loving structure of our home.

Late Teens Moving into Young Adulthood

As teens mature and move into the world as young adults, they begin to apply their knowledge to practical life skills. Debating the morality of curfew gives way to the practical application of knowledge such as budgeting, saving for big purchases, developing and maintaining long-term relationships, and using their time in a manner consistent with their priorities. They are preparing for living independently and making their own choices and assessing potential consequences (the pros and the cons) of various decisions.

Middle Age

As a person continues to move through adulthood, these practical matters become increasingly complex and involve more people. Daily struggles such as budgeting money for personal and family expenses, managing time for a spouse, children, parents, and in-laws as well as church and community activities, or managing the resources and dealing with the stress of caring for children and aging parents become priorities. Thinking and knowledge not only take on a more practical and immediate use, but expand to include the practical welfare of those we know and love.

Elderly Adults in Later Life

Aging—and specifically the problem-solving that comes with aging—brings wisdom. An elderly person often has a more long-term view of life and behaviors as well as a more systemic view of consequences. The elderly have extensive life experience in general, from years of experience in managing emotions and stress, and an accumulated mass of knowledge that leads to a new level of wisdom.[3] We can honor our elders by listening carefully to their wisdom. They offer us the gift of wisdom that can lead to understanding, discernment, and long life.

As you can imagine from the overview of developmental stages in the life-cycle presented above, how we honor a particular family member will depend, in part, on where he or she falls on the developmental continuum of thinking at a given time. Is their thought more concrete and literal or more abstract? Have they developed the ability to see things from another person's perspective, or do they continue to see things only from their own perspective? How much knowledge have they gained and have they begun to use it in a more practical manner? Take time now to consider each of your family members and how they think.

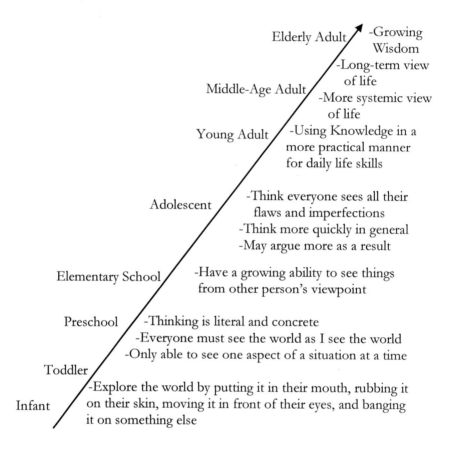

How Do They Relate to Others?

How a person relates to other people changes over time as well. For instance, an infant observes those around her to decide if the world can be trusted to meet her needs. The adults in her life honor her when they are consistent and responsive in meeting her needs without overindulging her. As parents honor her in this way, she learns to trust.

Once a child begins to walk, she must learn, with the assistance of her parents, to control her impulses and manage her emotions. A parent's loving discipline and playful interactions help her learn to manage her excitement and anger, curb her impulses, and exercise self-control.

The combination of loving discipline and playful interactions provides the sense of security she needs to develop a sense of independence. With a clear sense of security, she can begin to explore the world beyond her parent's side. Each excursion into the next room or to the other side of the yard is an adventure fraught with excitement and potential danger. As a result, she constantly looks to her parents, checking in with them, to confirm her own confidence and ability to explore safely, secure in her knowledge that her parents are not too far away. She may also demand to do things independently, making comments such as "No, I do!" as a way to assert and test her independence. As a parent honors her growing autonomy with encouragement and providing safe limits, she quickly learns what she can do on her own and gains the confidence to ask for assistance with those tasks she cannot yet complete on her own.

As a child continues to explore the world on his own, he discovers various tasks and activities that he enjoys. Preschoolers actively plan and create imaginative scenarios during play. It is a great honor to join a preschooler in imaginative play, whether it be with Barbie dolls or Spy Kids. Preschoolers may also experience frustration at not being able to complete a task the way they want to. At those times, parents can honor their child by encouraging him to ask for assistance and then offering that assistance without taking over and completing it for him or her. A parent who "takes over" when assisting the child dishonors the child. And, in dishonoring the child the parent interferes with their maturing motivation and hinders their growing initiative.

In elementary school, children not only enjoy the activity but desire to successfully complete the task, to be productive, and to master various tasks. Academically, they master reading, writing, and arithmetic. They also master complex social skills such as initiating interactions, making and maintaining friendships, pleasing teachers, and spending time away from family. At the same time, they begin to receive performance-based assessments from teachers and informal comparison-based assessments from peers. As a result, children often experience a slight drop in self-esteem during the first 1-2 years of elementary school. Fortunately, most children find success academically and socially, increasing their self-esteem until it levels off at an appropriate level. Parents honor their children by accepting their struggles, highlighting their strengths, allowing and encouraging them to contribute to the work around the house, teaching them to value and learn from mistakes, and creating rituals to make them feel special.

Teen years mark the struggle for personal identity and values. "Who am I?" "What occupation will I chose?" "What values will guide my decisions and life?" These questions, and others like them, become the compelling questions of identity during the teen years. Parents honor teens by allowing them to explore their identity while providing a safe and loving family structure. Talking about ideas rather than lecturing and giving ultimatums honors a teen and helps him think through his values and priorities.

When teens leave home, they continue to establish an identity in the "real world" of college or work (or both). Parents who have provided loving discipline and maintained close emotional ties enable their teen to successfully establish an adult identity and more easily move into the "adult world" of work and relationships.

What's more, relationships have a growing potential for lifelong intimacy during young adulthood. As a result, the feeling of rejection associated with "breaking up" can be devastating and call one's self-worth and identity into question. The strong support that understanding family and intimate friendships provide can buffer the emotional pain of such experiences.

Overall, young people struggle to develop intimate relationships, establish an identity in the adult world, and apply skills for living independently while transitioning away from the security and protection of home. This transition to adulthood is a major life-change that is filled with obstacles and stress. A young person whose family honors him with the security of loving and accepting relationships from which to explore and a safe port of understanding and support to which they can return in times of stress is truly blessed.

As young people successfully navigate their 20s and move through the adult years they find themselves working and raising a family. For the next 20-30 years, a person's life is filled with the joys and responsibilities of family life, the struggle to balance work and family, and the challenge of accepting an ever-evolving role in the changing world. Life experiences such as caring for elderly parents, watching children grow and leave home, negotiating a marital relationship as children are born, mature, leave home, and marry contribute to a greater understanding of the long-term effects of decisions and behavior. As a result, a growing sense of social responsibility emerges. People often develop a growing concern for guiding the next generation.

I find it interesting to watch pop stars move through life. Many of them live rather wild lives in their 20s. We hear of various stars in their late teens and early 20s being arrested for drug or alcohol abuse. We read media reports about how some decide to pose nude in magazines. As they mature and move into middle adulthood, however, the media reports change. We begin to hear how various stars are adopting needy children or "giving back" by sponsoring programs that support disadvantaged youth. We see them take a stand on pressing social and political issues and support those candidates and causes they believe will provide the best opportunity to impact the world in a positive manner. We read the children's picture books that they write as their attention turns to issues of parenting their own children. In essence, we watch them move into middle adulthood and act upon a growing concern for future generations and the world they will leave to the next generation (i.e., their own children and grandchildren). We can honor these stars, and indeed any person moving through adulthood, by accepting those changes and acknowledging their growing sense of responsibility.

As people move into the later stages of life, they tend to look back on their lives and review the things they have experienced and the choices they have made. They may recall good times with a sense of joy, sharing stories of adventure and excitement with friends and family. They may share stories of difficult times in which they express a sense of self-respect for successfully bringing loved ones through those difficulties. They also speak of mistakes and regrets, hopefully with a sense of self-forgiveness and as a way to help younger people avoid the same mistakes. As they share these stories, they gain a sense of fulfillment and integrity in their lives. They express comfort and satisfaction with themselves and those around them, accepting the good and the bad, the happy and the sad. With calm assurance they enjoy the final years of life. We honor them by listening to their life's story and acknowledging their wisdom, admiring their contributions, and learning the lessons of their lives.

This brief overview of development may help you look at your family members and assess where each is in life. In turn, you can better honor each of them with realistic expectations, respectful communication, and loving guidance that matches their developmental level. You can gain more information about any particular developmental area by consulting any of the many resources noted in Appendix A.

---

[1] One study met with toddlers, their mother, and a researcher. Together, they placed a crayon in a box. Then the mother left the room. The researcher and child conspired to move the crayon to a second box. When the researcher asked the toddler which box the mother would look in for the crayon, the toddler said the second box, even though his mother was not in the room when he and the researcher moved the crayon. He assumed that his mother would see everything the same way he sees it. Not until 4-5 years old did the children begin to realize their mother may see things differently than they do, and, as a result, would look in the first box, where she had last seen the crayon (Davies, 2004).

2 A child's brain overproduces neural connections and synapses (the network of connections between and among brain cells) as they move toward adolescence. At around 11-12 years old, the brain begins to "prune" those connections not used on a regular basis. As a result, the brain of the middle school child is actually undergoing a restructuring based on their relationships and experiences. This restructuring can contribute to what appears to be disorganized, absent-minded behavior.

3 Dr. Gene Cohen speaks of creativity and overall development in the elderly population. He uses the formula $C = ME^2$ to explain how creativity increases into old age. The "M" stands for the mass of knowledge that a person acquires over his lifetime. The "E^2" stands for the experience resulting in psychological and emotional growth as well as the experience that reflects accumulated life wisdom. This knowledge and experience combines to increase creativity and successful aging.

3 KNOWING THE ONE WE HONOR: 201

· ·

"There is depth of beauty and meaning inside [each member of your family] that will amaze you as you discover more of it. Enter the mystery with expectation and enthusiasm. Desire to know this person even better than you do now. Make him or her your chosen field of study, and you will fill your home with the kind of riches only love can provide."

–Stephen and Alex Kendrick, *The Love Dare*

I met my wife when I was 28 years old. We had a great time going out and learning about each other's interests and personality. One activity we both enjoyed was going to movies. Even though she enjoyed "chick flicks" and I enjoyed "guy" movies, we both enjoyed a good comedy or suspense movie. We also found that we both enjoyed bike riding and cooking out on a grill. We found many things we could enjoy together.

We also found areas of sensitivity—things that bothered her but didn't bother me and vice versa. We learned to become aware of those areas of sensitivity and "tread lightly" out of respect for one another.

We also found areas in which we simply differed. For instance, my wife is an outgoing person who loves to organize large social gatherings. I tend to be quieter and prefer quiet times with one or two people. She introduced me to a lot of great people and opportunities. I introduced her to quiet back-packing trips.

My wife likes to get work done before play. Not surprisingly, I tend to play before I work. I talk about buying things long before I ever do. If my wife talks about buying something, she will have done research and bought it by the end of the week. She often teases me because I will talk about taking a shower for about the same amount of time as the actual shower takes. The point is, we are different, unique, and special.

God, in His infinite wisdom, created us with differences. Sometimes we may think He made a mistake with our spouse, but He didn't. He had a plan in mind when He created each of us with unique qualities. He knew that because of those differences we could hold one another up and help one another grow. He knew that we could learn to value one another for the unique aspects of our personality and honor one another by using those unique qualities to help each other grow.

A wise man once instructed us to "train up a child in the way he should go" (Proverbs 22:6). The original language for the phrase "the way he should go" does not mean to train him up in the way we believe he "should be," teaching him right from wrong and enforcing proper behavior. Instead, the word used in the original language (Hebrew *pehderek*) means "according to his pathway; according to his bent." In other words, wise parents observe their child's personality, strengths, and natural curiosities and use that knowledge to train, nurture, love, and honor him (www.whatisgrace.org/sermonnotes/20080210_parenting6_faith.pdf). Although this proverb speaks specifically about parenting a child, I believe the principle applies to all members of the family. Carefully observing family members in order to better understand their personality allows us to better love, nurture, and honor them. But what do we look for when exploring personality?

Personality

Many factors impact our personality. For instance, we inherit a basic genetic wiring that contributes to a behavioral style. At the same time, our environment interacts with that basic wiring to shape our personality. Factors such as birth order and family relationships interact with inherited factors to shape our personality. Let's consider some inherited factors of personality.

Activity Level

One aspect of personality involves a person's level of activity. My two daughters have exhibited very different levels of activity from birth. My oldest daughter loved to snuggle and sit on my lap. She enjoyed long periods of quiet time snuggled up with me on the couch. My younger daughter, on the other hand, was much more active. She did not like to sit on my or anybody else's lap for long. She constantly looked around and explored her environment. As she grew older, she continued to move, even when she was engaging in a quiet activity such as watching TV or reading a book. My wife and I often wince at how she can contort her body while watching TV, twisting and turning her body while leaving her eyes focused on the screen and her feet unmoved. My daughters maintain different activity levels to this day.

Perseverance

Perseverance, a person's willingness to pursue an activity in spite of difficulties, influences personality. Some people persevere at a task in spite of obstacles and difficulties. Others lose interest at the slightest difficulty. I know an older gentleman who loves to fish. He endures what I consider amazing difficulties in order to cast a line in hopes of catching a fish. In the sweltering summer heat he would stand on the shore to fish. In the winter, he would drill through 3 feet of ice to fish in the bitter cold. He would rise early in the morning and fish until late at night, persevering long after I had given up hope that fish even existed in a particular body of water.

This perseverance was not confined just to fishing but played out in other areas of his life as well. He was born legally blind. His teachers did not believe he could graduate from high school because of his poor eyesight. He persevered, however, and not only proved them wrong but graduated as high school valedictorian. He went on to college where he also graduated valedictorian. Difficulties did not stop him from doing what he knew he could do. He persevered in spite of difficulties and succeeded in spite of obstacles.

Focused Attention

The ability to focus on an activity without interruption is related to perseverance. Some people can sit and watch the grass grow while others seem to need constant redirection to complete the simplest task.

My daughter loves to play and write music. When she writes a song she becomes very focused. Nothing distracts her—not hunger, not fatigue, not a ringing phone—*nothing*. She will even work on the song well into the night if we don't stop her. She becomes so focused on finishing the song that she doesn't notice when it's time for bed, time to eat, or time to take a break. My other daughter does the same thing when she reads. Once she begins a book, she becomes so intently focused on the book that she may not notice when it's time for bed, time to eat, or time to go to an appointment.

On the other hand, I have friends who seem to lose focus minutes after beginning a task. They have amazing abilities but often leave tasks unfinished because they got distracted by some other job that needed to be finished.

In between these two extremes rests a whole continuum of attention span and focus. Where do you fall on that continuum? How about your spouse? Your children? Which family members have an attention span similar to yours? Which have a different level of attention and focus? How does that impact your relationships? How does your attention span impact how you honor your family members? How can you honor your family members based on their attention span?

Adjusting to New Situations

How a person approaches and adjusts to new situations also affects personality. For instance, my oldest daughter tends to throw caution to the wind and dive into an experience. (Well, maybe I exaggerated some… after reading this story, you decide.) When my daughter was 2 ½ years old, she was the flower girl in a friend's wedding. She did a beautiful job. She marched down the aisle with confidence and poise. Later, at the reception, she was dancing and having a good time. As part of the reception tradition, the bride sits down and the groom removes the garter from her leg. The crowd gathered around the bride and groom. The music began to play. And, with a great show and frivolity, the groom began to remove the garter. Suddenly, the flower girl *(whose daughter is she anyway?)* broke from the crowd, sprinted across the dance floor, and tackled the groom. Playfully, the groom wrestled with my daughter.

As you can see, my daughter jumps right into new situations. I move slowly. I like to sit back and watch first. I like to practice and know what I'm doing and what I'm getting into. As a result, I start new things much more slowly and cautiously than my daughter.

Mood

Mood also impacts personality. You may have family members who always smile. No matter what is going on, they are happy. They always see the positive side of any situation and perceive the glass as "half full." At the slightest success, they throw a celebration. They jump up and down while shouting "Great job!" for even the smallest achievement.

Other family members may appear less happy or even somewhat melancholy. They may celebrate success with a simple smile and a nod of the head. At the extreme, they may struggle with periods of sorrow that were seemingly triggered by what others consider to be insignificant events. Along those same lines, some family members may act grumpy in the morning, others at night. Some may never act grumpy, smiling from the moment they jump out of bed to the moment they jump back in. In between these two extremes are an infinite number of variations, each having a different affect on personality and the way we honor one another.

Frustration Tolerance

Finally, how a person responds to frustration impacts personality. Some people become overwhelmed by frustration more quickly than others. I know a married couple in which each spouse has a very different level of frustration tolerance. Not long ago they were entertaining guests in their new home when the electricity went out. They ran to the window and looked out to find the entire neighborhood in the dark. The wife immediately got out some candles and began to talk with the guests. The husband became frustrated and worried. He began to wonder how long the electricity would be off, if the house would get cold, if the sump pump would quit and the basement would flood, if they would ever get electricity again or be found frozen to death in the morning. In his frustration, he did not want people opening the refrigerator door to let the cold air out or the house door to let the cold air in. All the while, his wife calmly reassured him and encouraged him to remain calm. Don't get me wrong. Both the husband and wife are lovely, kind, and compassionate people who simply respond differently to frustration. Both are successful and happily married. But they respond to frustration quite differently.

So What?

You may be wondering what this has to do with honoring family members. In presenting these descriptions, I pointed out some personality differences within my own family. Each family member is unique and different. These differences create the potential for conflict, sure. But they also create the opportunity to honor one another. For instance, when my daughter tackled the groom, I had a choice to make. The most honoring response would be to walk out in front of everyone, retrieve my daughter, and let the "show go on." But that goes against my personality, my tendency and desire to remain unseen and in the background at such gatherings. To honor my daughter in this situation, I had to step out of my comfort zone, walk out in front of everyone, and get my daughter.

As my daughter has grown, she has learned to honor my pace as well. For instance, she will ask me to join her in the swimming pool. After I agree to get in, she jumps in and starts to play. She enjoys herself as I prepare—very slowly—to "jump" in. I honor her by allowing her quick involvement, and she honors me by letting me become involved at a "slightly slower" (my daughter would say "painfully slow") pace. On occasion, I surprise her by honoring her pace enough to jump in quickly. In the end, we both have a wonderful time because we have honored one another.

As I noted at the start of this chapter, my wife is an extrovert. She loves to plan parties. She loves to get a large group of friends together to talk and play games. I am an introvert. I enjoy quiet times with about two or three people, maybe four. My wife graciously honors me by planning fewer parties at our house than she would like. She also helps to plan an activity night about once a month at our church, bringing a larger group of people together for food and fun. Even I enjoy those activity nights.

When she does plan a party, I participate. I move among the people, talking to a few at a time. If I feel overwhelmed, I just take a short break. Overall, I have a good time at the party. And I honor my wife with support while she honors me by accepting my need to "get away" sometimes.

Family

These personality traits interact with many environmental influences. For instance, birth order influences personality. Whether a person is born first, last, or somewhere in the middle influences his strengths, weaknesses, outlook on life, and interaction with the world. Take the first-born child, for example. First-born children have the opportunity of being the only child for a short period of time. As a result, the first-born receives the attention of an only child. His parents notice everything. As younger children arrive, he has the responsibility and pressure of being the oldest and, presumably, most responsible child.

I teach a few classes at a small college near my home. In one class, I generally ask which students are first-born and which are later-born. As we discuss birth order, the first-born students adamantly state that they "weren't allowed to do anything" whereas their younger siblings "got away with murder." They believe that their parents were "harder on them" and had more expectations of them than they did for their younger siblings. Maybe they are on to something there. Since children do not come with a training manual, parents learn through trial-and-error. And, the first-born (lucky child) has the privilege, and pressure, of teaching new parents to parent.

For instance, new parents often have unrealistic hopes and dreams for their children. The first-born may find himself frustrated trying to live up to these unrealistic expectations, pressured to bring honor to the family name. Since this is the parents' first experience with a child of their own, they may also overreact to accomplishments and mistakes, adding additional pressure to the first-born child.

When other children are born, the firstborn is old enough to help. So they get some responsibility: "Go get you brother's binky, please." "Will you get me a diaper, please?" "Be a good example for you sister." If you have been a parent, you know how this list can grow as we seek help getting everything done. Not only does the assistance help us, but it presents an opportunity to intentionally teach our oldest child to be a responsible helper. Unfortunately, it also adds to the pressure on the first-born to be a "good" child.

This environment has benefits. It often leads the first-born to become a responsible and competent achiever. The first-born also tends to become reliable and achievement-oriented. They tend to uphold the status quo of the family while seeking the approval of their parents and other adults.

On the other hand, they can become controlling and perfectionistic. Still, approval remains important. You can imagine how being a perfectionist can interfere with one's ability to recognize the approval that others give or the ability to give approval to others at times. It can also lead to some apprehension and fear of "stepping out" into the unfamiliar.

Middle-born children have the unique advantage of an instant playmate and role model. They immediately look up to their older sibling and want to do everything that their "older brother/sister" does. Even so, middle-born children have to find a different place in the family from that place their older sibling occupies. Generally, the first-born sibling is an achiever, so the second-born child becomes the social child. Since the older sibling generally wants to maintain the status quo of the family, the second-born may disrupt that status quo.

Interestingly, if the second-born child is not the last child, he will have the additional experience of having an older sibling and a younger sibling. From this middle position, he will gain firsthand knowledge both of how an older sibling perceives things and how a younger sibling sees things. This gives middle children the opportunity to learn the art of peacemaking and negotiation. They may devise creative solutions to resolve problems and disagreements. In addition, middle-borns often allow stress to simply roll off their backs. They often appear unaffected by stressors or the perceived disapproval of their parents. But they find great value in the approval of their peers. As extremely loyal friends, they may sacrifice their own opinion, or compromise their true desire, in order to keep the peace.

The youngest child also has instant playmates and role models. They do not know what it's like, however, to have a younger sibling. They are the "baby" or "princess" of the family. Parents and siblings provide affection and care for the youngest child's various needs and often treat them with "kid gloves." In addition, last-borns often learn to "do their own thing" with fewer restrictions and at a younger age than their older siblings. They love to be the center of attention and often use their charm to convince others to do things for them. Indeed, they are charming, fun-loving, and happy go lucky. After all, other family members have already assumed responsibility for family functioning, allowing the last-born to focus on fun and adventure. Spontaneity becomes their *modus operandi*, often combined with significantly less achievement orientation or self-discipline than the first-born child. At the same time, they can be charming, affectionate, and loving.

What does birth order have to do with honoring family members? We honor our family members differently depending on their birth order. For instance, we might honor the first-born by letting him know that we appreciate his accomplishments. Family members might honor a middle-born child by listening to him and encouraging him to give honest, heartfelt input. Families can honor the last-born by teaching him to take responsibility and allowing him opportunities to do so. In addition, you can honor the last-born by acknowledging his loyalty and learning to "let go" once in a while to have fun with him in a spontaneous manner, an especially hard task for the first-born.

Our birth order also provides an opportunity to express honor to family members in unique ways. For instance, if you are a first-born, you can honor others by not competing all the time and not setting the bar so high. Honor family members by letting them shine, get attention, or take the lead, even if it "goes against your grain." You may also honor family members by apologizing, an especially difficult task for the first-born. The middle-born child might honor family members by becoming vulnerable enough to give honest, heartfelt input rather than simply giving in to everyone else's desires. Honor your family by allowing them to know you deeply as you express your true desires and emotions. The baby of the family can honor other family members by taking on various responsibilities in the house and seeing that another family member gets to enjoy being the center of attention.

I'm sure there are many other ways to honor one another based on birth order. Take time to consider each of your family members' birth order and how you can honor each as a result. If you desire to learn more about the impact of birth order on relationships, consult the resources listed in Appendix A.

Love Languages

Ty and Tayona came into my office concerned about their marriage. As we spoke, a common conversation ensued.

> *Tayona:* I don't think Ty loves me anymore. He never wants to spend time with me. He never says he loves me.
>
> *Ty:* What are you talking about? I go to work every day. You don't think I do that for myself, do you? I do that for you…to make life better for us, so you can have nice things. And what do you mean we never spend time together? We spent all afternoon together last Saturday.
>
> *Tayona:* Ty, we watched the football game.
>
> *Ty:* But we were together. I enjoyed our time together. I guess *you* don't like spending time with *me*.
>
> *Tayona:* Yes I do. I want time with just you and me. And I'd rather have you home more and making less money if that meant we could spend time together. I don't need you to make money.

The conversation went on, but you get the drift. In reality, this couple loved each other. They really did want to express love to one another, but their efforts were mis-communicated. Tayona wanted Ty to show her that he loved her through spending quality time together. Ty was showing love by bringing home gifts. They both loved each other but didn't know how to communicate that love in a way that the other would understand. Ty and Tayona spoke different love languages—meaning that each communicated love in different ways. In a sense, one spoke French and one spoke Chinese, and neither understood the other. Ty and Tayona could honor one another by learning to speak one another's love language.

What are love languages? Gary Chapman (2004) suggests that there are five love languages: words of affirmation, quality time, receiving gifts, acts of service, and physical touch. Not all family members will speak the same love language. In fact, family members will most likely speak different love languages, giving us unique opportunities to honor one another.

Words of Affirmation

Chapman (2004) suggests that some family members speak "words of affirmation" as their love language. They feel loved when they hear verbal compliments or encouragement. Compliments and words of appreciation communicate love in powerful ways. They communicate that we notice the other person and his or her efforts. Encouragement communicates a personal interest in the other person. It communicates that we have taken the time to learn about what is important to him and that we are with him, available to help if it is desired. Expressing love through "words of affirmation" demands that we speak kindly. A soft answer, a kind compliment, a word of appreciation, or loving expression of encouragement can speak volumes of honor and love to our family members who speak this language.

Quality Time

Other family members may recognize love through "quality time" spent together. Spending quality time involves focusing all of our energy on the other person for a period of time. It may include quality communication about experiences, thoughts, feelings, and desires in an uninterrupted context. It is giving our undivided attention to the other person. Quality time allows people to express themselves to one another openly and know that they are listened to. This kind of intimate conversation may occur while sitting at a romantic restaurant or walking through a quiet neighborhood in the evening. Either way, it represents a period of uninterrupted time in which all your attention is focused on the other person and your gift of time spent with him or her.

Receiving Gifts

"Receiving gifts" is another way that people can feel loved. People who speak this love language do not necessarily desire big expensive or extravagant gifts. Any gift, even small gifts, becomes an expression of love and devotion. The gift reveals that you thought about the other person, that he or she was in your mind and your heart even when not by your side.

Acts of Service

"Acts of service" is a fourth love language. Doing simple chores can become an act of service that expresses love for the one who speaks this love language. Taking out the trash, doing the laundry, or loading the dishwasher can become a way to honor a person with your time, effort, and energy. If your family member speaks this love language, find out what "acts of service" are most appreciated. Do it out of love and honor rather than a sense of guilt or obligation. Let the service reveal the kindness and love in your heart.

Physical Touch

Finally, some family members need "physical touch" to feel loved. Hugs, back massages, a touch on the shoulder, or a gentle slap on the back may communicate love to the person who speaks this love language. A simple act of touch can communicate deep honor and love. You don't want to embarrass a family member through physical touch, so, study your family members to learn what type of touch they find most expressive of love. Consider what type of touch may best communicate love to your family members.

That is a very brief overview of Gary Chapman's five love languages (2004). Learning how your family members experience love—what says "I love you" most effectively and satisfyingly—can provide you with many opportunities to honor them in special ways. You and each of your family members could learn your primary love language by taking the "30 second assessment" at www.fivelovelanguages.com. You can also learn more about the love languages by reading the books listed in Appendix A.

4 KNOW THE ONES WE LOVE: 301

. . . .

I have friends and acquaintances who love football. They watch all the games even if they have to record a game so they can watch it later. They know the players' names, backgrounds, and achievements. They can often recite players' position, height, and weight. They can rattle off statistics about a favored player's style of play and perhaps even tell you the names of the player's wife and children. Don't get me wrong. There is nothing wrong with loving football or any other sport. We all have hobbies and activities we enjoy. Some of these men, though, have trouble telling you the name of one of their own children's friends, even though they live with the child. They have difficulty recalling their anniversary date, even though they see their wife everyday. They have no mental model of their family members' lives or personhood. When this happens, football becomes the symptom of a much deeper issue, an issue of priority and honor.

We tend to make time to learn about those things that we love and value. We spend time being with and learning about the things we value. We talk about the things we love. If we want to honor the members of our family, we need to learn about them. We need to pay attention to the details of their lives and become intimately familiar with their world. Basically, we need to learn each family member's stats.

Here is a list of questions to help you begin learning the statistics for your family members. Go through them to see what you know and don't know. Some of the questions relate to the information from the previous two chapters. Others questions deal with other ideas. If you want, you can play a little game with these questions. John Gottman (1999) has a list of question he calls the "love map game." He suggests that each person ask other family members a set number of questions about himself. The other person answers. Each correct answer scores two points. An incorrect answer scores only one point. High score wins. Really, everyone who plays this game wins as we learn about one another and grow closer together.

If you do not want to make it a game, make it part of daily small-talk with your family. Ask family members a few questions each day as you talk together throughout the day. OK, let's get down to business and learn the family stats.

Name: _____ Birthday: _____ Age: _____

1. How does she think? Is she able to take another person's perspective?

2. What is/was her favorite subject in school? What interests her?

3. How does she relate to others?

4. Does she jump into new activities or enter cautiously?

5. Does she like activities that involve a lot of physical activity (like sports) or more sedentary activities (like reading) or a little bit of both? Is she always on the go?

6. Does she like to "work now and play later" or "play now and work later"?

7. How well does she persist at and focus on tasks? How long is her attention span?

8. Is she a generally happy person? How emotionally expressive is she?

9. Does she prefer interacting with large groups of people, or does she prefer a quiet, intimate party with two or three others?

10. Who are her current friends? Are they the same friends as she had in the past?

11. Who are his friends' parents? Brothers? Sisters?

12. What activities does he enjoy with his friends?

13. How often does he enjoy activities with his friends?

14. Who are his potential friends?

15. Does she/he have a boyfriend/girlfriend? What is his/her name? What kind of person is he or she?

16. Who are his biggest rivals or competitors? How are they rivals?

17. Who does he trust/mistrust among his peers?

18. What is he looking forward to?

19. What are some current stresses in his life?

20. What does he worry about?

21. What are her dreams and aspirations?

22. What is her favorite kind of music? Music group?

23. What is her favorite TV show?

24. Is there something she would like to change about herself? If so, what?

25. What kind of books does she like to read?

26. What was the worst event in her life?

27. What does she like to do when sad? Happy?

28. What personal changes would she like to make in her life?

29. What makes her feel most confident and strong?

30. What are her hobbies? Interests? Recreational activities?

31. What is he afraid of?

32. What was his favorite vacation?

33. How does he like to be soothed or comforted?

34. What is his favorite sport?

35. What is his favorite food? Next favorite food?

36. What is his favorite color?

37. What is his favorite movie?

38. What movie would he currently like to see?

39. Who does he most admire? Who are his heroes?

40. What is he good at? What are his strengths? What are his exceptional abilities?

41. What activities and hobbies most interest her?

42. What would she do during a day in which she could do anything she wanted to do? What would be her perfect day?

43. What are her talents? How does she like to be encouraged in those talents? What are her dreams regarding those talents?

44. What does she like best about her body? What does she like least about her body?

45. What function of her body most amazes her?

46. How much rest does she need to function optimally?

47. What is she like if she misses a meal? How does food impact her energy level and mood?

48. How does she relax?

49. Does she have any allergies?

50. How does she manage transitions and changes?

51. What makes him laugh?

52. What is he passionate about?

53. Where is he in his relationship with God?

54. What makes him feel loved? What is his love language?

55. What is his biggest fear?

56. Other points of interest.

5 THE FAMILY BANK OF HONOR

....

"We are called to honor someone even when we know all too well
their deepest character flaws. We are called to stretch ourselves,
to find out how we can learn to respect this person with whom
we've become so familiar."

–Gary Thomas, *Sacred Marriage*

You have now honored the members of your family by taking the time
to learn about them. You have invested the time and energy necessary
to become intimately acquainted with their world and you have developed
a more in-depth mental image of their lives. You have learned the stats for
each family member. In so doing, you have laid a foundation of honor.
Now you can build on that foundation to create a home of honor.

We recently had to replace our front porch. The old one was pulling
away from the house. The gap between the porch and the doorway was
becoming a canyon. Parents feared losing small children in the chasm
and adults had to take a leap of faith to get over the chasm and in to our
home. So we hired a contractor to tear out the old porch and build a new
one. In our community, that also meant obtaining a zoning permit and
a building permit. Though we had been saving money for about a year,
having to withdraw money from our savings account to pay for a new
front porch was still frustrating. We had made deposit after deposit into
our savings account over the previous year and had finally built up a small
savings. Then we had to replace the porch. After a solid year of faithfully
making deposits into our savings account, a single withdrawal took our
savings back to ground zero. Isn't that the way it always happens? Multiple
deposits are lost with a single withdrawal.

Honor is like that. We make deposits into the family bank of honor
when we practice daily acts of honor and over time build up a nice honor
account. But the one time we act dishonorably (and we all have those

times) we make a huge withdrawal. The hope is that we have made enough deposits of honor, both great and small, to maintain a positive balance in the family bank of honor even when we have these honor lapses.

John Gottman (1994) found that happy couples have 5 positive exchanges for every 1 negative exchange during an argument. He also noted that "master couples" have as many as 20 positive experiences for every 1 negative experience when they are not fighting. In other words, happy couples have at least 5 more positive feelings and interactions than unhappy couples. This information gives us the basis for a formula of honor banking. We need to make deposits into the family bank of honor every day, at the rate of *at least five deposits (acts of honor) for each withdrawal (act of dishonor)*. With this ratio of deposits to withdrawal, we begin to build a home environment of honor. But the question remains: Exactly how do we make a deposit of honor?

Accept Influence from Others

One way to bank honor is to allow your family members to influence you. Popular culture does not encourage accepting influence, especially for males. Instead, we are taught to "fight for our rights" and "assert ourselves" and "stand our ground." We strive to become people of power who can influence others rather than humbly accepting the influence of others. Unfortunately, an attitude that emphasizes *my* rights and strives to make *my* influence known at the expense of others results in major withdrawals from the family bank of honor.

To make deposits into the family bank of honor we must accept the influence of others rather than demanding our own way. We need to listen to our family members and accept how they think and feel about a given topic. Ask for their opinion and advice even if you think you know better. Jesus did this. Recall how He asked Philip where they would get the money to feed the crowds before He fed them with the five loaves and two fishes (John 6:1-14). Peter's great confession—"You are the Christ, the Son of the living God"—occurred during a discussion in which Jesus asked the disciples what the people were saying about Him and who the disciples believed him to be (Matthew 16:13-17). Surely Jesus knew what the people were saying about Him, but He asked the disciples anyway, to invite them to participate with Him and share that moment.

My daughter enjoys music and is a talented musician. Sometimes when we sing together she will say, "Dad, you're not singing all the notes right." I have to confess that when this happens my first impulse is often frustration. I feel offended and want to defend myself. If I become angry and defensive, I dishonor her by denying and belittling her influence. And, in doing so, I damage our relationship. She becomes frustrated that "I never listen" and, in turn, I become more defensive: *Why does she always criticize me?* We argue. In frustration, we end our music session for the day on unpleasant terms. If that pattern repeats, we may quit playing music together altogether. What a shame! We would lose a wonderful opportunity to enjoy one another's company and grow closer all because I refused to honor my daughter by accepting her influence.

On the other hand, if I respond with honor by accepting her influence, we can discuss which notes she thinks I missed. And, 9 times out of 10, I can learn about a mistake I have made and correct it, thanks to her willingness to bring it up. As I honor her by allowing her to teach me, our skills increase. She becomes a better music teacher and my pitch gets better. More importantly, though, it is our relationship that gets better and grows more intimate. She feels listened to and valued. She learns that her input is important and meaningful. We continue to play together and enjoy our precious time together. We add wonderful deposits into our family bank of honor.

Even When We Disagree?

Accepting a family member's influence becomes more difficult when you disagree. It's easy to cast blame, criticize, and maneuver the conversation to "win" the argument and "make them" understand rather than accept their influence. We sometimes simply give the *appearance* of listening as we are in fact formulating our arguments. We may not like to admit it, but most of us want to save face by proving our point when we disagree rather than accepting the other person's influence. We would rather be admired for our power in proving a point than to humbly "give in" to the other person's influence, even if it means creating distance in the relationship. We want to be the influencer not the one influenced…especially during a disagreement.

Building relationships of honor, however, demands that we humbly accept one another's influence. Accepting influence during a disagreement means not only listening intently to understand the other person's point of view but making sure the other person *feels* understood as well. Disagreements resolve more quickly when everyone involved feels accepted, listened to, and influential in the other person's life. Disagreements resolve more quickly when we honor one another enough to acknowledge the other person's ideas and build on common ground rather than simply beating out the areas of disagreement. Overall, we make huge deposits of honor when we accept one another's differences and work together to find solutions.

My Own Little World

Some people miss the opportunity to accept influence because they live in their own world. They become so caught up in work or hobbies that they do not think about their family members. Rather than accepting influence from family members, they make passive attempts to satisfy the family without ever stepping out of their own selfish world.

Joe was like this. He passively agreed to go on a family picnic while concentrating on work papers. When the day of the family picnic arrived, his family began making preparations. His wife and children packed the picnic lunch. They gathered their swimsuits and toys. They put on sun tan lotion and were all ready to go. Just then, Joe said, "Oh, the picnic's today, already? I was making a work call. Hold on, I have one more call then I'll be ready." For the next hour, everyone waited while he made that one more call, changed his clothes, and tied up loose ends for work. You can imagine how frustrated his wife was with his lack of concern for their plans. Unfortunately, she unleashed her frustration on the children when they misbehaved because they were restless waiting for their father. When the father was finally ready to go, he found a frustrated and angry family sitting in defiant silence.

Joe was so caught up in his own world—the world of his work—that he did not fully listen when his family tried to include him in their plans. He failed to recognize the hustle and bustle as his excited family prepared to go on the picnic. By focusing solely on his own world, he missed the opportunity to accept his family's influence. In so doing, he had made a huge withdrawal from the family bank of honor when he had a rich opportunity to make a pretty big honor deposit. Even worse, his withdrawal contributed to further withdrawals that left the family bank of honor overdrawn and family members angry.

But Sometimes I Am Mad

Accepting influence does not mean that we never express negative emotions. Relationships benefit when family members listen carefully, accept one another's opinions, and work to create a positive solution in order to resolve conflicts (Gottman, 1999). In fact, honorable disagreements make deposits into the family bank of honor. We will discuss how to have honorable disagreements in the next chapter.

Overall, accepting influence from other family members enhances the positive aspects of the relationships. Accepting influence reveals an underlying love and respect for one another. It assures the other person that he is accepted "warts and all." It communicates that you truly value your family members and that they are very important to you—so important, in fact, that you are willing to listen to them and follow their counsel. It builds relationships and communicates that "we are on the same team and in this together, no matter what." Accepting influence makes huge deposits into the family bank of honor.

In the Christian life we call accepting influence "being subject to one another in the fear of the Lord" (Ephesians 5:21). Christ led by example in accepting influence as a way of honoring others. We gain a glimpse of how He accepted the influence of others when Luke tells us that He "continued in subjection to them [his mother and father] ... increasing in wisdom and stature and in favor with God and man" (Luke 2:51-52). Jesus apparently accepted the influence of His earthly mother and father as well as other earthly authorities during his childhood.

We also know that Jesus "emptied Himself" in obedience to His Heavenly Father and took the form of a servant (Philippians 2:7), a man under the influence of others. Notice the verbs in Philippians 2:7-8. Jesus *"was made* in the likeness of man" and, *"being found* in appearance as a man."* In both cases, the passage implies that Jesus was passive; He was accepting the influence of His Heavenly Father. On the other hand, He *"emptied* Himself and *took* the form of a bond-servant." This shows that Jesus was active in emptying Himself; no one else did it for Him. Thus He actively pursued the role of a servant. When God revealed Himself in Jesus Christ, He chose to do so through a servant, a servant who actively *took* that role.

Through no choice of their own, children "find themselves" born into their family. Although they did not choose their family, they can choose to accept the influence of that family.

Adults can also "find themselves" in the role of spouse or parent. They can drift into the role of spouse without making any active choice along the way. What begins as an initial attraction and some casual dating drifts into spending a night together once in a while. That "once in a while" grows to three or four nights a week because the drive home is long or both partners are tired. The nights spent together slowly increase until the couple drifts into living together, perhaps in an effort to share financial expenses. Suddenly, a baby comes along, and, to give the baby a family, they marry. So these two people "find themselves" in the role of spouse and parent.

Other people actively decided to marry but, when the honeymoon ends, they "find themselves" in marriage quite different from the one they had imagined. Like Jacob in the Old Testament, they thought they had married Rachel only to wake up one day and discover they are married to Leah. Isn't this what happens to all of us to some extent? We "find ourselves" in a marriage or family at least somewhat different from the one we had imagined. Those endearing traits of the "Rachel" we married give way to the irritating behaviors of "Leah." Then children enter the picture and we experience a whole new level of discovery. We "find ourselves" "being made" into the role of parent and spouse in a family that just does not quite—or at all—measure up to the fairytale we had imagined.

No matter where we "find ourselves," we follow Jesus' example by "emptying" ourselves and "taking the role of a servant" in relation to our family. We should actively pursue the role of a servant—one who accepts the influence of others—in our family.

I am not saying that you need to accept influence to the point of accepting abuse or death or doing something that clearly goes against God's will. Rather I am just pointing out that even Christ accepted the influence of His Heavenly Father, His earthly parents, His peers, and the earthly authorities of His day. In fact, He actively pursued a role that demanded that He accept the influence of others. Recalling His willingness to accept influence helps me to do the same.

Holding One Another in Mind

I used to equate the fifth commandment—to honor our parents (Exodus 20:12)—with simple obedience. Honor, however, involves much more than mere outward obedience. It involves keeping our parents' concerns, interests, sensitivities, and desires in mind so that we can willingly accept their influence in our lives. Keeping our parents in mind not only allows us to accept their influence but enables us to identify many other ways to show them kindness and love throughout the day.

This holds true also for honoring all family members, not just our parents. When we keep the concerns, interests, sensitivities, and desires of our family members in mind, we become aware of many ways to honor them. If we do not hold our parents, spouses, or children in mind, we pass up opportunities to honor them and, perhaps worse, we do not even become aware of those opportunities. We skip blindly past opportunities to honor them because their concerns, interests, and desires are not important enough for us to give a space in our lives and minds.

On the other hand, when we hold our family in mind, we become aware of various ways in which we can serve them and perform kind deeds for them throughout the day. When we hold our family in mind, we are more likely to take our dirty dishes to the kitchen and wash them rather than leave them in front of the TV for someone else to clean up. We are more likely to put our shoes away rather than leave them in the middle of the floor for someone else to trip over.

Family members know that you have them in mind when you remember them in little ways throughout the day. For instance, calling to check in throughout the day lets the other person know that you "keep her in mind." I often have to leave early in the morning before my wife and children get up for the day. So when I know they are awake, I call home to "check in." I usually spend a couple of minutes talking with my wife, then each of my daughters. The conversations are short, but it lets them know that I am thinking about them. They learn that they occupy an important place in my life, my heart, and my mind, even when we are not together.

Asking family members about their day or the things they value reveals that you have kept them in mind. Asking about the test they took, an activity they attended, a friend who was hurt, or a particular concern lets them know that you keep them, and what is important to them, in mind. It reveals that you believe their world and life are important and want to know more about them. It reveals how much you value them.

We also mark special events in the lives of those we value and hold in mind. I remember an incident early in my relationship with my wife. We had known each other only for about five months when I promised to take her out for her birthday. A month later, when her birthday arrived, I had forgotten. On the day of her birthday, I was excited to cook her dinner. I kept pondering why she appeared upset as I set the table for her and set out the "gourmet" chicken I had prepared. Finally, she told me that it was her birthday. I felt terrible. She felt terrible. I had not honored her by keeping her and her birthday in mind. And I learned a valuable lesson about honoring someone enough to keep her in mind.

We have to make a choice to hold each of our family members in mind. If we do not make a conscious effort to hold them in mind, something else will fill our mind and force our families out of mind. We can either train our mind to dwell on our family members or allow "other stuff" to passively fill our mind. To make no choice will result in passively allowing "other stuff" to fill our minds.

I have met several men who love their wives and families but do not keep them in mind. They did not train their minds to dwell on family and, over time, "other stuff" fills their mind—such as text-messaging other women and entering chat rooms while on the road for work. These men could not explain why they started relationships on-line, but I suspect that part of the reason is that they did not hold their wives in mind. To put this another way—if we do not hold the precious diamonds of family in mind, coal will take over.

Keeping family in mind may take conscious effort at first, but the dividends are well worth the effort. For instance, you might write a reminder to call your family in your appointment book (or set a reminder on your Outlook calendar). You might program birthdays, anniversaries, and special events into your Blackberry. Put pictures of your wife and children in visible places in your car, office, or the hotel room you stay in while traveling. Whatever it takes—keep your family in mind.

In summary, you honor the people you value by holding them in mind. And you further honor them with deeds of kindness, words of encouragement, and acts of service as you discover opportunities throughout the day that lead you to think, "My wife/husband/child would like that!" We can keep one another in mind by remembering special events, special interests, areas of concern, and particular sensitivities. By keeping one another in mind, we communicate a sense of "we" rather than "me." We reveal that family members are not in this alone, but that "we" are all in this together. We communicate that each family member is important enough to remember and valuable enough to hold a space in our mind throughout the day, even when he or she is not physically present.

Speech that Honors

Richard Halverson, Former Chaplain of the U.S. Senate, has noted that we can offer ideas as "bullets or seeds." I believe his quote reflects the nature of speech as well. Read his quote now as I modified the original by changing the word "*idea*" to "*words*":

> "You can offer your *words* to others as bullets or as seeds. You can shoot them, or sow them; hit people in the head with them, or plant them in their ears. *Words* used as bullets will kill inspiration and neutralize motivation. Instead as seed, they take root, grow, and become reality in the life in which they are planted." —Richard Halverson

Mr. Halverson knows the potential power of words to crush or encourage.

The old saying "sticks and stones may break my bones but words will never hurt me" is just not true. Words have tremendous power. They can build up or tear down. They can serve as deposits into the family bank of honor or withdrawals from the family bank of honor. They can mend a broken heart or crush the spirit. They can draw people together or tear them apart.

Words become seeds or bullets in the heart of those to whom we speak. Ancient Hebrew wisdom noted that shooting the bullets of negative words can destroy a neighbor (Proverbs 11:9) or crush the spirit (Proverbs 15:4). But planting the seeds of positive words can make the heart glad (Proverbs 12:25) and offer healing (Proverbs 15:4; Proverbs 16:24).

The Scriptures tell us to speak only those words that are good for edifying one another in the moment, giving grace to all who hear (Ephesians 4:29). The one who receives words of edification also receives a benefit. Those same words, however, give grace to everyone who hears them spoken. Don't you feel encouraged when you hear a man use his words to edify his wife? As we speak words of edification and encouragement to our family members, we create an environment in which words are used to honor. As a result, everyone benefits.

Scripture also tells us to let our speech be gracious, "seasoned as with salt" (Colossians 4:6). Isn't that a beautiful thought? Like salt, gracious speech brings out the true flavor of honor. Our gracious words create a thirst for more gracious words and encourage others to use similar gracious words. As parents speak gracious words to their children, their children thirst for more gracious words and learn to love the flavor of gracious words. As a result, they are more likely to continue the tradition of speaking gracious words to their parents. Like salt, gracious words also preserve the honor of the speaker as well as the honor of the one spoken to.

How we speak to one another offers a simple way of making multiple deposits into the family bank of honor throughout the day. We can offer words of encouragement and praise. We can speak words of thanks and gratitude. We can speak to one another with gentleness and kindness. Each time we speak gracious words, we make deposits into the family bank of honor.

One special way to honor family members with our words is through a testimonial (Seligman, 2002) or blessing (Smalley & Trent, 1993). This exercise presents a wonderful opportunity to honor family members with words. Here's how to do it: Think of one of your family members and the characteristics that make him or her special to you. What do you admire about her? What do you appreciate? Think of two or three attributes and a specific example to support each one. Write these attributes and the related examples on a sheet of paper or a greeting card. Then arrange a time to meet with that family member. Ideally, you read the short testimonial to her and then give it to her to keep. After sharing the testimonial, enjoy your time together. If you have ever received such a testimonial or blessing you have experienced firsthand the honor it brings to the recipient. And if you have ever given a testimonial to someone you care about, you know the honor you feel in giving the blessing away.

The Honor of Sacrifice

Couples with the happiest marriages exhibit a willingness to sacrifice for one another (Markman et. al., 1994). When we are willing to sacrifice our own interests for our family members, we honor them. We are "emptying" ourselves in order to show them the extent of our love. Sacrificing for one another implies that:

> "…with humility of mind [we] regard one another as more important than [our] self; not merely looking out for [our] own personal interests but also for the interests of others" (Philippians 2:3-4).

Sacrificing for one another person reveals the value and importance we place on him or her. It honors the other person.

When we hold family members in mind, hundreds of opportunities arise each day to honor them through simple sacrifices. For instance:

- Listening to your child tell a story rather than watching your favorite TV show or sporting event
- Volunteering to do a chore around the house that is actually another family member's job
- Letting a brother or sister sit in the chair, or the preferred seat, rather than fighting over it
- Holding the door open for your wife
- Unlocking the car and opening the door for other family members before getting into the car yourself
- Running an errand for a family member when you would rather sit on the porch

- Letting one of your family members have the last piece of cake or the last cookie or the last *anything*
- Listening to another family member's choice of music in the car rather than your own

You get the idea. Every day is packed with little moments that provide big opportunities to make hefty deposits into the family bank of honor. Start each day with a commitment to keep your eyes and heart open to see the doors of sacrifice and walk through them to honor your family members with little acts of kindness and loving sacrifice.

You may also have the opportunity to make bigger, more costly, sacrifices, even though some such sacrifices will go unnoticed by some family members. For instance, some parents choose to sacrifice their own career for a period of time in order to raise their children. Why? Because they place greater value and honor on their children than on their own career and income-earning potential. Every year men and women choose to slow the advance of their career during their childrearing years, sacrificing the immediate pay-off of getting ahead in their career advancement for the sake of their family—to help their children get ahead. Adolescents may sacrifice time with a friend—even a cherished boy or girlfriend—in order to go on a family vacation. These significant sacrifices, and others like them, bestow great honor on other family members. They require that we put "skin in the game" and cost us something, but the payoff is a large deposit in the family bank of honor. And, even when no one else is aware of the sacrifice, I believe that God will see and honor that sacrifice. After all we know that God "gives grace to the humble" and "exalts them in His time" (1 Peter 5:6).

Honoring Achievement

Families also make deposits into the family bank of honor by celebrating one another's achievements and accomplishments. This can be as simple as celebrating a milestone such as a birthday or anniversary or an achievement such as completing the school year or sports season. No matter what achievement you celebrate, remember a few key points:

(1) **Celebrate** the effort not just the final product. If a child earns a "C" grade but put in excellent effort, celebrate the achievement and the hard work! If the baseball team lost but played a hard game, celebrate the effort and the grit! Let family members know that effort—not just the outcome—is

admired and honored. The goal is not just to win or achieve the perfect score but to put in our best effort. So, honor effort with celebration.

This also applies to honoring the effort made to change behavior. Sometimes a person engages in a behavior that irritates other people in the home. As family members complain (and speak the truth in love), the person honors the family by making the effort to change that behavior. If other family members do not acknowledge that effort, it may just be that the negative behavior actually received more attention and energy than the new positive behavior. In a sense, the negative behavior received greater honor in the form of attention while the positive behavior was dishonored by a lack of recognition. If this is the case, the honored negative behavior will increase while the dishonored positive behavior will decrease.

We can honor the new positive behavior by acknowledging the effort put forth to change. We can praise the family member for demonstrating the desire to change and for every step he makes toward that change. We honor him by letting him know that we see and appreciate the effort.

(2) Honor differences. In a home of honor, family members accept one another in spite of differences and even honor one another because of those differences. Many couples who admired one another for their differences while dating find, after a few years of marriage, that those differences have become points of irritation and dishonor. What was admired and honored as spontaneity while dating may be seen a few years later as irritating disorganization and lack of planning. What was admired and honored as an inspiring ambition and organized desire for success while dating may be seen as a rigid and blind drive to achieve later on. That "wonderful conversationalist" somehow becomes over the course of a few years "one who never hushes up for a minute to let somebody else get word in edgewise." So often what initially attracted us to someone repels us later on. What a wonderful opportunity for giving honor!

If you find yourself becoming irritated with the differences family members exhibit, learn to think of the irritation as a signal to practice honor, just as needle on E on the gas gauge signals the need to fuel up. No need to get angry at the signal, just recognize it as a signal and take action. In this case, take a little time to think about any potential positive aspect of the behavior rather than immediately criticizing it. Then acknowledge and express gratitude for the positive aspect of the behavior to honor your family member (Gottman, 2001). Perhaps an example will help make this clear.

When I first met my wife, I admired her organizational ability. She is an excellent organizer. This translates into a neat house in which everything has a place. So when we married she kept an organized home. If I can't find something, she knows exactly where it is. It's amazing! On the other hand, when my wife and I come home from a date, she immediately starts picking up the toys and clothes our children left on the floor. I am ashamed to say that on more than one occasion I became irritated when she started cleaning. I wanted to sit down on the porch and continue our evening of quiet conversation. "Why can't she just sit down and relax with me for a minute?" I thought. "Cleaning the house is more important to her than spending time with me." My irritation was a signal to practice honor.

So instead of complaining I eventually took the time to realize how much I appreciate her efforts to keep a clean home and how much effort she puts into caring for our children. Instead of grumbling about my initial irritation of her "rigid need for order," I honored her by helping to pick up the mess. I further honored her by telling her I appreciate what a good mother and housekeeper she is and ask if we could sit and talk after we finish picking up. And just like that my irritation became an opportunity to honor my wife and develop intimacy with her—and both of our needs got met.

What have you done for me lately?

In 1986 Janet Jackson asked "What Have You Done for Me Lately?" The song basically goes on to ask why her lover was not as attentive as he once was. He was not honoring her the way he used to honor her. Perhaps she was asking the wrong question, though. If we want to become a catalyst of honor in our families, we need not ask "What have *you* done for *me* lately?" Instead, we need to ask, "What have *I* done for *you* lately?" What opportunities did I see and act upon to make a deposit into the family bank of honor? Did I seize the opportunity to develop intimacy with my family members?

Everyday, family members make efforts to connect with one another through touch, facial expressions, or playful behavior. They may attempt to connect through words, gifts, or acts of service. Sometimes the attempt is clear; other times it can be subtle and less clear. As we honor family members by learning more about them, we become more aware of their "style" and mannerisms when attempting to connect. For instance, knowing one another's love language can help us connect in meaningful ways. We can use the awareness gained from learning about one another to honor each other's efforts to connect by responding with energy and attention, encouraging further efforts to connect and build intimacy.

So, what have you done for your family today? What deposits have you made into the family bank of honor?

6 TO HONOR IN CONFLICT

"Making someone else feel smaller so that we can feel larger is antithetical to the Christian faith, a complete rejection of the Christian virtues of humility, sacrifice, and service. So often Jesus left the crowd to minister to the individual, while we rationalize leaving the individual—particularly our spouse—to carry favor with the crowd."

–Gary Thompson, *Sacred Marriage*

Honoring our family is easy during the good times. When conflict arises, however, my true level of honor is tested. It becomes difficult to honor a family member when I feel misunderstood or when I find myself disagreeing with someone. How can I honor my children when I have to discipline them for some misbehavior? How do I maintain honor in the midst of an argument?

If you have followed the advice of the previous chapters and become a student of your family members, developing a complete mental image of their unique characteristics and world, and made daily generous deposits into the family bank of honor, you will find it much easier to maintain honor during conflict. You will find yourself and your family members primed to honor one another.

Still conflict is inevitable. It's not a matter of *if* we will have conflict with family members but rather *when* we will have conflict. Unfortunately, some of the most damaging actions and statements occur in the heat of conflict when our anger burns hottest and our selfish pride bares its teeth in order to save face. Our words can become bullets and our decisions can become bombs that disrupt relationship. We say and do things in the midst of conflict that we would never even consider saying or doing outside of conflict. If we are honest with ourselves, we have to admit that in the midst of conflict there is grave potential for hurting one another and damaging our relationships.

On the other hand, conflict can actually strengthen relationships—if it is resolved and managed with honor. Marriage experts such as John Gottman (1994) report the benefits of having and resolving disagreements. For instance, some degree of conflict may fuel desire and help keep passion in a marriage. If resolved successfully, conflict may also promote long-term health in a relationship by weeding out actions and behaviors that, if left unchallenged, might harm the marriage or family.

Honoring a person with whom you have a conflict, although not simply a conflict-management strategy or a discipline strategy, does help protect the relationship over the long term. Honoring a person during conflict communicates an unconditional love that helps to nurture and protect the relationship in the midst of conflict. Let's explore some ways to honor our family members in conflict.

Quick to Hear

The first step in honoring a person during conflict is to listen intently. If you are quick to hear, conflict provides you with an opportunity to know the other person better. Listen with the purpose of understanding the other person and his perspective. Conflict arouses emotions, and emotions reveal areas of sensitivity and priorities. In this way, conflict opens the book of the other person's heart and soul, revealing his fears and priorities. The actual words and pattern of the conflict are merely the cover of the book. We have to look beyond the cover and listen to (read) the story to find the sensitivities and priorities that fuel the response. Seize the opportunity of conflict to listen carefully, to read the open book, and to discover the other person's priorities or sensitivities.

José shared with me a comment he had made that angered his wife. Seeing a pile of cat hair by the chair he had remarked, "We had better clean up, I guess." His wife accused him of being rude. She thought he was implying that she was a poor housekeeper. He explained that he meant merely that they needed to clean the room. José and I considered the underlying message of her anger and the priority and sensitivities it revealed. He realized that his wife was sensitive about the house and felt the need to be seen as a good housekeeper. With that in mind, he could then honor his wife by communicating, in words and actions, his appreciation for her efforts in the house. By being quick to hear, he learned about his wife and areas in which he might encourage her on a regular basis. He learned how to build his wife up rather than engage in a conversation that would bring them both down.

Many times, especially in conflict, we do not listen to understand. Instead, we listen only closely enough to gain information that will help us prepare our opposing response. As a result, we hear only part of what the other person is truly saying and miss vital information as we contemplate our counterargument. If we listen only enough to gather ammunition for our response, we continue filtering everything through our view of the argument and never really understand the other person's perspective. We will only become further entrenched in our own position and dig in our heels. And the words we speak from that position will surely be bullets fired to destroy rather than seeds planted to grow closer in our relationship. We may also make judgments about the correctness or accuracy of what the other person says without ever taking the time to fully understand his position and feelings.

Pride is what makes us believe that our own point of view is more important than the other person's point of view. When we put more effort into making the other person understand our point of view than we do trying to understand his point of view, nothing good is going to come of it. This approach stands in opposition to Paul's words in Philippians 2:3-4:

> "Do nothing from selfishness or empty conceit, but with humility of mind let each of you regard one another as more important than himself; do not merely look out for your own personal interests, but also for the interests of others."

Honoring a person during a conflict demands that we humble ourselves enough to listen—*really listen*—without interrupting or imposing our own point of view. Honoring a person during conflict involves listening empathically, striving to understand what the person means and feels to the point that we can explain her perspective and feeling about the issue at hand. This will demand not only hearing what is said but how it is said. It is not just hearing the words but listening to voice quality and body language as well. In fact, most communication is non-verbal, meaning it falls outside the realm of mere words and includes tone of voice, volume of voice, and body language. So we must listen not merely with our ears but with our eyes and heart as well while seeking to understand the other person's feelings, intent, and perspective. Notice that we seek a *complete* understanding, not just knowledge of the words spoken, but a complete understanding of the underlying emotion, intent, meaning, and purpose of the communication. This deep level of understanding, which is so rare in our world of shallow chatter, truly honors the other person.

I often hear couples get caught up in the words of the disagreement. They haggle over this word or that. Perhaps you have done this, too. I know that I have. Instead of recognizing the emotion expressed in my wife's total communication, I focus on the words she chooses to use. Instead of empathizing with her, I filter her words through my understanding of the issue, my fear of conflict, and my prideful desire to be right. Then I become angry about a particular phrase she used because I mistakenly perceive those words as casting blame on me. If I would only take the time to listen, really listen, I would hear and see more than the words she used and, instead, pay attention to the emotion in the whole of her communication. That humble awareness would allow me to come to a more complete understanding of her intent and what she really means. I can respond to her total communication based on an understanding of her perspective of the situation, her needs, her emotions, and her desires. Maybe for just a moment I can really see the situation as she sees it and feel it as she feels it. If I do, I will come away changed.

Such empathic listening not only honors the other person but often reduces the intensity of the conflict as well. It turns down the heat. As we come to more completely understand the other person, we can appreciate her perspective and respect her thoughts. We can step into her shoes, so to speak, in order to have the discussion, in much the same way as God stepped into our shoes to become a man in Jesus Christ (Philippians 2:7). Because He took the time and effort to experience life from our perspective, He can speak for us as a merciful and faithful high priest (Hebrews 2:17), sympathizing with our weaknesses (Hebrews 4:15). Amazingly, He honored us in this way while we were still in conflict with Him (Romans 5:6-10)! Likewise, we are called to honor those family members with whom we have conflict by seeking to fully understand them and to communicate that understanding to them. Above all, we do this by listening intently so that we might understand.

Slow to Speak

Honoring a person while in the midst of conflict also demands that we speak carefully. Words spoken in the heat of conflict carry extra power. They penetrate more deeply into our minds, hearts, and sense of self. So do not jump into the conversation prematurely and "shoot off your mouth" (remember those word bullets). Instead, listen intently to completely understand the other person's perspective and, then, only then, speak carefully.

John Gottman (1999) has noted that "96% of the time you can predict the outcome of a conversation based on the first three minutes of the fifteen-minute interaction! A harsh startup simply dooms you to failure." To honor family members, we must speak gently, not harshly. This includes being appreciative, polite, and clear in our conversation. Describe what you see happening rather than evaluating or judging. Don't check the Golden Rule at the door when you are in conflict: Treat your family member as you want to be treated in your communication. Keep your speech kind. Do not call names. Do not become critical or engage in character assassination. Don't make statements that jump from a complaint about behavior to demeaning comments about the other person's character.

For instance, imagine a wife and husband who disagree about the amount of supervision their 4-year-old son needs during play. The husband wants to let their son play in the back yard with his older siblings. His wife disagrees and voices her concerns. Unfortunately, as she is speaking, her husband continues helping their son put on his jacket to go outside. He does not look up at her. So he does not see the worry in her face or hear the concern in her voice. As the husband finishes tying their son's shoes, his wife says, "You just don't know anything about children. What kind of father would allow his child to play unsupervised and risk wandering away?" With that comment, she moved the disagreement into an argument and used a word bullet to assassinate her husband's character. She no longer spoke with kindness. He was not merely doing something that could expose their son to risk (a behavior) but he was a bad father (character).

She could have said something such as, "I know you love our son, but I'm still concerned. What if he falls down or wanders away? I think he needs more supervision at this point." This would have led to a different discussion with a different outcome. Instead, she made an accusation about his character as a parent and even called into question his concern for his son. The husband was not blameless in this ill-fated conflict. He could have stopped readying their son and looked at his wife as she spoke and listened intently to the meaning behind her words. He would have recognized her concern and worry and, with that knowledge, responded to her concerns rather than merely stating facts about the yard and forging ahead with his own agenda. He had dishonored her by not listening intently. She had dishonored him by speaking harsh, unkind words that belittled his character and knowledge.

Nothing good can come of this kind of exchange. It makes a huge withdrawal from the family bank of honor.

Keep in mind that words spoken in the heat of a conflict burn into the heart and mind of the other person. Like quick drying cement, they quickly harden into rigid patterns of thought that can result in either honor or dishonor. Do you want the words you say in anger to encourage thoughts that promote honor or dishonor? Let's consider three examples of potential patterns that can produce honor or dishonor in conflict (Seligman, 1995).[1]

One morning, John and his wife found themselves arguing about the toothpaste. In anger, John yelled, "Why can't you just squeeze the toothpaste from the bottom of the tube? You ruin *everything!*" I realize that in a calm mood that statement sounds utterly ridiculous. But when we do not honor one another during a conflict by being "slow to speak" we often make such ridiculous comments. In this case, in the course of a single sentence John jumped from the specific issue of the toothpaste to a global issue of *everything*. John accused his wife of "ruining everything," not just his experience of brushing his teeth. She squeezed the tube of toothpaste differently. That was the issue that ruined the whole world. Once again, this type of approach will only exacerbate the argument, leaving John's wife with little response but to defend herself, counterattack in kind, or shut down. The issue of the toothpaste will never get resolved because it got lost in the dishonor communicated by global accusations.

John could have said, "Honey, could you please try squeezing the toothpaste from the bottom? Otherwise the toothpaste is messier and we waste a lot when we can't get all of it out." Notice how John maintained the specific concern in this statement. The issue was about the toothpaste—not about everything. He softened it with a term of endearment ("Honey"), which says I love you and we're in this together. He did not dishonor his wife by an epic overreaction that suddenly claimed that she "ruins everything." This statement is kinder and more accurate. It leaves room for continued discussion and possible resolution.

As the argument continued, John yelled, "You *always* think you're right, don't you? You *never* listen to me!" When John calms down, he will likely be able to recall several incidents in which his wife has listened to him. He will realize the inaccuracy of his accusations. The trouble is, he has already dishonored his wife with this false accusation; and, because he stated it in such superlative and permanent terms, he has left no room for further discussion. If she "never" listens, what is there left to talk about? John and his wife are at an impasse. His wife will likely defend herself. She will point out all the times she has listened to him. The argument will most likely escalate—who knows where it could go from there?—but the initial topic will be lost. Instead, the argument will now focus on a much more volatile and provocative topic: respect and honor, the accuracy of perceptions, the quality of character, and the permanent or temporal nature of her ability to listen. The temporary issue has been lost in the dishonor communicated by accusations of permanent, negative behavior.

Eventually, John's wife becomes so angry that she says, "John, you are so selfish, just like your father: *rigid and mean.*" She has made a statement about his personal character—and his father's! She has made the external concern about toothpaste an internal character fault. How can he change if that is his internal nature? He is stuck being selfish, rigid, and mean. Once again, the argument escalates as John feels the need not only to defend himself but his father as well. As the argument escalates, the minor issue related to toothpaste gets lost in the dishonor communicated by accusations of an internal character flaw (and one that even runs in the family).

Of course, this is a silly example. You can see clearly, however, that we can honor or dishonor someone by what we say during an argument. Do we make the conflict a permanent issue with them or a temporary incident? Do we keep the conflict about a specific issue or "pull in the kitchen sink" to make it about *everything?* Do we blame the conflict on the other person's internal character flaw or consider what external factors may be influencing the situation, including our own contribution? Do we make accusations about the other person's internal character or lovingly request some behavioral change?

Honoring a person during a conflict demands that we keep the conflict specific to the temporary incident at hand and consider each person's contribution as well as the contributions of other factors in the situation. Let's compare the statements described above within the context of a conversation and consider a more honoring alternative.

Dishonor	Honor
John: "Look at this toothpaste. It's ruined!"	
John's wife: "What are you talking about?"	
John: "Just look at it. You just squeeze it anywhere and now it's a mess, ruined!"	

John's wife: "Who cares? What's the difference?"	
John: "I care, that's who. Why can't you just squeeze the toothpaste from the bottom? Why do you have to ruin everything?" (global)	*John*: "Why can't you squeeze the toothpaste from the bottom? It's neater and you waste less toothpaste that way" (specific and request behavior change)
John's wife: "What are you talking about? It's just toothpaste. I can squeeze it any way I like."	
John: "You always think you're right, don't you? You never listen to me!" (permanent)	*John*: "I suppose you can. I told you why I like to squeeze from the bottom, why are you so opposed to that." (temporary)
John's wife: "I do, too. I always have to listen to you complain about this, complain about that. I'm tired of listening to you whine about everything." (global)	*John's wife*: "I'm not *so opposed* to it. It's just that…I don't know. You sounded so bossy and I got mad. Sorry."
John: "Oh yeah, now it's *my* fault. You're such a jerk. It's never you're fault, is it?"	
John's wife: "You are so selfish, just like your father, rigid and mean!" (internal character fault)	*John's wife*: "You seem really upset. Is there something going on, something bothering you? You don't usually say stuff like that. It hurts my feelings. Please don't do it anymore." (explore external cause and request behavioral change)

Intersperse the honoring statements above with attempts to de-escalate the conflict and you have a couple who is honoring one another during conflict. Attempting to de-escalate the conflict puts the brakes on a discussion that starts down the icy road of endless accusations and negative statements. We can put on the brakes to de-escalate the conflict and help turn it around by making what John Gottman (1999) calls "repair attempts." These repair attempts honor others by decreasing the tension and lowering the stress of everyone involved. They honor the people involved and the relationship they share. Repair attempts can range from a silly inside joke to a serious heartfelt apology, from the simple and quiet, "Hmm, I hadn't thought of that," to the loud, but sincerely spoken, "Well, I'm sorry!"

Let's revisit the toothpaste battle between John and his wife and insert some repair statements as well.

> John: "Look at this toothpaste. It's ruined"
>
> John's wife: "You sound pretty passionate about your toothpaste. Sorry [repair attempt], I didn't know you cared that much."
>
> John: "Well, I do. I mean, maybe I'm a little over the top [repair statement], but I don't want to waste any—we can't afford to waste any."
>
> John's wife: "That's fine. I appreciate your concern for our money [repair statement]. I'll work on squeezing the bottom. I was a little nervous though; I thought you were going to take my head off over the toothpaste."
>
> John: "Sorry [repair statement]. I guess I went a little overboard."
>
> John's wife: "Overboard? I think you abandoned ship [repair statement]. Anything going on?"
>
> John: "Well, I've been kind of stressed...."

In this scenario, the couple honored one another in using repair attempts. They quickly resolved the initial conflict. What's more, they moved on to deeper and more substantial concerns that allow them to become more intimate with one another. What could be more honoring?

Repair attempts work best when both people involved in the conflict are committed to honoring one another. One person has to honor the other enough to put on the brakes and humbly make a repair attempt. The other person has to honor enough to hear the repair attempt and respond to it. A foundation of honor, built by becoming a student of one another and making daily deposits into the family bank of honor, supports the walls of respect and friendship that will increase the effectiveness of repair attempts.

Slow to Anger

If you have established an environment of honor by becoming a student of each family member and made daily deposits into the family bank of honor, you will find it easier to slow your anger and not "blow up." If during the early stages of conflict you have listened intently, spoken gently, and honored your relationship by putting on the brakes, you will find your anger greatly reduced. You will find that you become less critical and feel more loved and respected. You will find that you become less defensive and better understood. As you hold the value of family members in mind, you will discover a growing desire to understand them. You will find yourself feeling safer and less in need of withdrawing to protect yourself.

Of course, you may still experience anger, but you are more likely to balance that anger with love and honor. One of the first things you can do to honor your family member in the midst of your anger is to *take a step back*. Many times I meet with couples who have described intense arguments filled with anger. When I ask them what started the argument they cannot remember. They recall only the intense emotion. Perhaps they could have avoided the escalating tension by simply taking a step back.

"Step back" long enough to calm down and regain control of your emotions and actions. This may involve thinking about something other than the source of the argument, doing some physical exercise, taking a shower, or working in the garden. Do anything constructive that will help you regain control of your emotions and allow you to return and converse calmly and lovingly about the topic at hand. This honors your family member and sets the stage to resolve the disagreement in honor.

Christ tells us to "take the log out of your own eye, and then…the speck out of your brother's eye" (Matthew 7:5). In other words, take a look at yourself. Before we can honorably resolve conflicts and disagreements, we need to assess our own contributions to the conflict. You cannot change the other person. You can only change yourself. So before you try to explain, justify, or defend your actions, make a private, honest assessment of your motives, goals, and expressions.

Consider your contribution to the current conflict. Take time to think through why *this particular topic* at *this particular moment* evokes such strong emotion in you. Reflect on what you can learn about yourself from this situation.

Think about any ways in which you instigate or perpetuate the conflict. Do you have unrealistic expectations or did you make any unrealistic demands? Did you engage in any name-calling or did you withdraw your love, attention, or involvement during the argument? Did you become defensive and, if so, how did that defensiveness impact the conflict? Do you tend to blame your family member for the conflict and, if so, how does that impact the conflict?

As you step back and explore your own emotional response to this conflict, think about what you can learn about yourself. Our anger in conflict often hides a deeper fear and insecurity. The intense emotional response of anger within a family often hides a fear that the relationship is threatened. On the other hand, the intense emotional response also reveals the strong desire for, and the priority placed upon, a sense of security and a desire to connect.

As you realize the core fears and hurts of your own emotional response, realize that your family member is probably feeling similar emotions. They, too, experience fear when the relationship is threatened. Your family member also places a strong priority on a sense of security and a desire to connect. Consider how you can help meet that need in her life, even as you work to resolve your current disagreement.

Once you have stepped back, calmed down, and taken the "log from your own eye," you can return to your family member with a renewed calmness. Together, you can honor one another while resolving your disagreement. In the process of resolving your disagreement, you can show one another compassion, realizing that the other person hurts just as you hurt. You can honor him with any apology that might be necessary, such as apologizing for hiding your true needs behind anger, blaming, or withdrawal.

You can also honor your family member by "believing the best" (1 Corinthians 13:7) about him—believing that he truly does have the intent of creating a more loving, intimate relationship. Confirm your love for him, reassuring him that you love him in spite of any anger he expresses.

Throughout this process, you have honored your family member. This process can help you use the energy of your emotions to accomplish the goal of resolving the differences and reestablishing your relationship. In the midst of the conflict and working toward resolution, you can honor the other person by remaining aware of how he responds to your statements and his facial expressions, making adjustments that will assure him of your love and commitment. If you see that your response to him is only increasing his anger, fears, or insecurity, you can quickly repair that damage and make further deposits into the family bank of honor.

[1]Martin Seligman (1995) describes three attribution styles that contribute to optimism, pessimism, learned helplessness, and even depression. These attribution styles describe patterns of thought that we have in response to situations. The patterns of thought include thinking about situations as either:

- Specific or global
- Temporary or permanent
- External or internal

Attribution styles are learned; which means that we can change them as well. One of the major contributors to which patterns we learn is how the authorities— i.e., parents and teachers—speak to us in the midst of heated interactions such as disagreements, conflict, or discipline. The patterns we learn impact our self-confidence, mood, and perseverance. So when we experience negative conflict, we want to keep our focus on the specific problem versus pulling in the "kitchen sink," the temporal nature of the problem versus making it a permanent issue, and look for possible external contributors along with requesting specific behavioral changes rather than diagnosing the other person's internal character flaws.

7 HONOR AND DISCIPLINE

"Disrespect is the weapon of the weak."

–Alice Miller

"Misbehavior and punishment are not opposites that cancel each other; on the contrary, they breed and reinforce each other."

–HaimGinnot

Webster's New World Dictionary (1980) defines discipline as "training that develops self control, character, or orderliness and efficiency." This definition focuses on "training that develops" certain desired characteristics. It does not mention punishment, which Webster (1980) defines as "a penalty imposed on an offender for a crime or wrongdoing." Discipline may include some punishment, but punishment does not constitute effective discipline. Even though discipline and punishment are clearly not the same thing, many families act as though they are. Consider some of the differences.

- Punishment attempts to reduce negative behavior by imposing a penalty. Discipline trains us to live out a positive life-style.

- Punishment points out what we do wrong but it does not teach us appropriate alternative behaviors. Discipline does teach appropriate alternative behaviors.

- Punishment reduces negative behavior only when the external risk of punishment remains. Discipline, on the other hand, strives to build an internal desire to do the right thing in any circumstance.

- Punishment encourages a person to become "sneakier" to avoid getting caught. Discipline encourages a person to grow in self-control and positive character.

- Discipline honors a family; punishment, in and of itself, does not.

In order to teach self-control, godly character, and an orderly life, family members must honor one another with discipline just as God disciplines His family.

Our Example

The writer of Hebrews tells us that God disciplines His family "for our good, that we may share in His holiness." In other words, God promotes positive self-control, Christ-like character, and orderliness through discipline. He disciplines those He loves to promote their growth in the Christian life. God's discipline helps us learn to live in a way that pleases Him and brings the "peaceful fruit of righteousness" into our lives. In God's family, discipline and love go together and result in holiness, peace, and righteousness (Hebrews 12:6-11). In a similar manner, discipline honors our family by growing the "peaceful fruit of righteousness" among family members.

The Flow of Discipline

We often think of discipline within the family as moving from parent to child. Loving parents discipline their children in an effort to help them mature and become contributing, respectful members of society. Discipline, however, does not flow only from parent to child. It flows between all family members, nurturing the whole family. Each family member trains other family members in "self-control, character, or orderliness and efficiency." For instance, children train parents in patience, self-control, love, humility, courage; how to handle anger in a godly manner; and to more carefully define, and act upon, priorities. These traits sound very much like self-control, character, and order. If we, as parents, do not grow in these characteristics through the lessons we learn while parenting our children, our children will not likely learn the lessons we hope to teach them.

Our spouses also train us. Among other things, our spouses train us to forgive, to manage our anger in a godly manner, to love deeply, to think about others more than ourselves, to behave kindly, to disagree graciously, and to give sacrificially. As we accept this discipline and grow in response to it, our marriages grow stronger and more intimate.

Discipline flows throughout a family in formal and informal ways, adding structure and security to family life. Discipline honors the family.

Handling a Work of Art

The intentional Christian family strives to discipline in love not in anger (especially uncontrolled anger). Families that discipline in anger do not honor family members. Instead, they treat family members like the seed of Satan rather than a precious creation of God. Intentional Christian families, on the other hand, remember that each family member is a child of God, a work of art created in His image. Recognizing one another as one of God's masterful works of art helps us to discipline one another in love.

Scripture tells us that wives are priceless vessels to be honored as "fellow heirs" (1 Peter 3:7). Husbands are to treat their wives with gentle, loving honor as they work to grow more mature in Christ together. In general, our spouse is our spiritual equal not our student. She or he is a priceless creation of God whom we honor by treating as such.

I believe the same principle holds true in regard to children. Although parents are to lovingly discipline their children, they are also warned not to provoke their children to anger (Ephesians 6:4). I have seen many parents manipulate their children with guilt or rage rather than shape them with loving discipline. They provoke them to anger rather than train them in love. The disrespect in this approach becomes even more apparent when we realize that our children do not belong to us alone. As God's creative masterpiece, they ultimately belong to Him. When we manipulate and provoke them, we disrespect God's gift and, ultimately, the Gift-giver Himself. When we discipline with His ownership in mind, we honor both our children and God.

In summary, loving discipline honors the whole family, treating each member as a carefully crafted gift from God. Through loving discipline, families promote self-control and godly character in each family member. Such discipline honors God and His family.

Words of Honor

The results of discipline will reflect the disciplinary process used. Said another way: Discussions about behavior will end in the same manner they begin. If we want the discussion of discipline to end with honor, we must begin with honor. If discipline begins with uncontrolled speech such as sarcasm or name-calling, it will end in further disrespect, uncontrolled speech, and dishonor. If a discussion about problematic behavior begins with honor and love, it can more easily end with honor and love. In other words, effective discipline utilizes speech that honors the other person as a gift from God. At least four ingredients will add honor to our speech during discipline.

1. *A "soft start up" (Gottman, 1999) shows honor.* Avoid sarcasm and speak gently. Avoid accusations of bad character; instead, focus on the *specific* behavior you want to change. Rather than claiming the behavior is permanent, "always" occurring or "never" changing, point out how the person can choose to behave differently the next time.

2. *When giving verbal discipline, keep it brief.* I have watched family members simply shut down and quit listening to spouses or parents who did *not* follow this simple principle of honor. As they go on and on about some behavior they do not like, family members simply quit listening. They no longer hear the complaint and they do not learn any new behavior. Instead of learning self-control, they witness a lack of self-control. Rather than growing in character, they learn to shut others out in anger. They learn to act dishonorably. To express honor in our discipline, keep it brief.

3. *Listen to understand rather than debate to be understood.* By way of an example, I often do an exercise involving 5 brief discussions to help people learn to listen and discuss disagreements rather than debate. We begin by having a short discussion in which we constantly make unrelated responses to one another. If they talk about pizza, I bring up the weather. If I talk about sports, they talk about school. Obviously, this type of conversation easily becomes frustrating. Family members engage in this type of response when they become so focused on their own agenda that they do not honor one another by listening.

   In our next discussion, we constantly disagree with one another. If they say it is a nice day, I respond by saying something like, "No it is not. It is too cold." If I say they have a pretty shirt, they respond by saying, "This old thing is so ugly, I wanted to throw it away this morning."

As you can imagine, this conversation often ends with frustrated silence. We dishonor one another by constantly disagreeing and restating our point rather than listening to understand the other person's point of view.

In the next conversation we respond with a "Yeah, but" to every comment. You know the conversation. "It is a beautiful day." "Yeah, but the wind is cold." "Yeah, but the sun is nice." "Yeah, but the bright light hurts my eyes." "Yeah, but…." I'm sure you have had those conversations. Like the previous two conversations, this one invalidates and disregards the other person rather than honoring them.

Next, we begin each response with a "Yeah, and…" "It is a beautiful day." "Yeah, and the wind is a little cold." "Yeah, and the sun is nice." "Yeah, and I think I will wear my sunglasses." This conversation goes much more smoothly and honors the other person's statement by at least listening to what they have to say.

The last conversation offers the greatest level of honor. In this conversation, both parties listen intently enough to hear and repeat what the other person has said. Only after the speaker feels understood can a response be offered. In the midst of teaching self-control and positive character, this conversational style becomes most honoring and effective. It teaches listening and elevates the other person, validating his or her worth. It begins with the intent of understanding the other person and will more likely end with being understood.

4. *Do not make threats.* Threats do not honor families but tear families apart. When I worked in community mental health I would often hear parents say, "I'm going to call child welfare and tell them to take you away." Similar statements include: "Maybe we should just get a divorce" or "I'll leave and never come back" or "Fine, I'll never ask you again." Such threats produce deep pain and hurt. They damage relationships. In addition, they hide the underlying feelings. A more honoring

approach would be to vulnerably offer up the deeper feeling—
"I'm scared I might lose you," "I love you too much to let you
behave this way," or "It hurts me to see you suffer, but I know
this will help you later."

If you follow these few suggestions, you will have a very different
experience of discipline—an honoring discipline—from what the world
has to offer. This type of discipline shows respect and love for others and
treats them as the precious gift from God that they truly are. It looks past
any temporary discomfort to envision the long-term maturity of the other
person. Throughout this process of loving discipline, both parties honor
one another by maintaining and restoring their relationship.

According to the Individual

Each family member will respond to different types of discipline based
on their personality, age, and position in the family. Families honor one
another by holding each family member's unique personality in mind when
they discipline. For instance, one of my daughters was very sensitive to
discipline when she was young. If I gave her "the look," she knew she had
done something wrong and would often begin to cry. I had to be careful
not to use too harsh a tone of voice or become too loud when I disciplined
her because she was so easily overwhelmed. A simple look was all it took
to get her to a more appropriate behavior.

My other daughter, on the other hand, was much more strong-willed
as a child. I could give her the same look—"*the* look"—and she would
simply smile, wave, and say, "Hi Dad." When I told her what she had done
wrong, she would simply stare blankly into my eyes. Many times I had to
take her by the hand and explain in detail what she had done wrong, why
it was wrong, and what behavior we expected in its place. She understood
and would make changes; but even then she would simply smile and say,
"OK." Each one had her own personality and each responded to a different
style of discipline.

Believe All Things

Most of us know 1 Corinthians 13:7: Love "bears all things, believes all
things, hopes all things, and endures all things." But do we really apply this
when it comes to our discipline? When we discipline, do we truly believe
that the other person has a desire to change and will attempt to change?

I remember reading a story about two teachers. Both were very strict, gave tons of homework, and kept students very busy throughout the class time. They differed only in their expectations of the students. The first teacher gave tons of homework in the belief that "I know I'm hard on you, but it is because I know you can do it." This teacher enjoyed the love and respect of her students. Her students were successful and well-behaved.

The second teacher kept the students busy because she had the expectation that if she did not "keep these kids busy they will stab me in the back." Students in this classroom did not perform as well. Instead, they misbehaved more often and the teacher was constantly punishing misbehavior and trying to gain control (Wasicsko & Ross, 1994).

Students and family members alike pick up on the subtle behaviors that reveal our beliefs and expectations about them. And they tend to act in response to those beliefs—living up or down to others' expectations. If we believe that our family members are "bad," we will treat them accordingly. For instance, we will constantly warn them against bad behavior, perhaps becoming a nag. We may also be on the lookout to catch them doing something wrong or stand guard lest some misbehavior slip by unpunished. This constant focus on negative behavior inadvertently rewards it with attention; and, rewarded behavior increases. As the rewarded negative behavior increases, we may begin to feel that our belief about their "bad character" has been confirmed. "See, I knew it—he's a bad kid, a real sneak." In our mind, they have fulfilled our low expectation of them and given us proof-positive that we were "right." In response, we find ourselves growing more frustrated as they continue to live down to our low expectations.

Of course, if we believe they really want to change and grow, we will treat them accordingly. For instance, in a family based on honor and love, most people will want to behave in a manner that maintains positive relationships. When we work to create that type of family and believe that family members want to do the right thing as a result, we are more likely to treat them with kindness. Treating our family members with kindness increases the likelihood of receiving kindness in return. This translates to fewer behavior problems. In addition, we will be more likely to look for positive changes and acknowledge those changes as they occur. Once again, *rewarded behavior increases*. Rewarding positive changes with attention leads to more positive behavior. In other words, our family will more likely live up to our high expectations.

Here are some ideas to help you act on a belief that family members desire to change and grow.

1. *Rather than telling family members what to do or what they are doing wrong, ask them questions:* Is that the way we act in our family? Are you sure that is the best response? Do you think that will help you get what you want? Such questions encourage the person to think about her actions. They encourage the person to search her memory for the priorities and values she has been taught. Such questions also send the implicit message that you believe that she knows the answer and really wants to live within the family parameters and values. Of course, this step does imply that those values have been clearly spoken and taught. If not, this is an excellent time to calmly discuss family values and the reasoning behind them.

2. *Give choices.* Rather than simply telling someone what to do or how to behave, offer a choice. Sometimes the choice can represent two positive outcomes. For instance, "That shirt is in the wash. Would you like to wear this shirt or finish washing the other shirt?" Other times, the choice may be to behave appropriately or accept the consequence. Of course, you have to be willing to accept the person's choice and then follow through with the consequence. For instance, "You need to clean up your room before you go. If you do not, you will be grounded for the rest of the weekend."

3. *Make a family effort to provide undivided attention to positive behavior and godly character.* You can do this by offering praise and thanks to one another. Praise and thanks are excellent ways to promote growth and maturity. In many families, negative behavior gets more attention than positive character. It is easy to energetically respond to inappropriate behavior in an attempt to change it. Unfortunately, this attention may just reward and increase the behavior (because rewarded behavior increases). Instead, calmly respond to negative behavior with discipline. Give the negative behavior very little energy, while energetically attending to positive behavior. Responding to positive character and appropriate behavior with energetic attention, recognition, thanks, and praise will promote those behaviors we desire.

4. *When you praise, praise specifics.* Instead of saying, "that's a beautiful picture" offer a more specific praise such as "I love the colors in that sunset. You really picked a wonderful shade

of orange." Notice the colors used in a craft, the effort put into a project, the spirited or sensitive performance of a piece of music, or some other specific aspect of a completed chore. A specific praise carries more weight. The other person knows that you really paid attention to what he did rather than simply gleaning enough information to offer a cursory praise (also known as "damning through faint praise": "Isn't that *nice?*"). In addition, a specific praise opens the door to further discussion and deeper relationships.

5. *Don't praise and qualify.* Qualifying praises are comments such as "That's a good paint job *for you*," "At least this meatloaf is better than the last batch you made," or "This room looks *pretty* clean…if you want to live in a pig sty." When we honor someone with praise, we simply offer the compliment without qualification. We may go on from the praise to lovingly point out areas of continued improvement, but let the person enjoy the praise. Doing so communicates our belief in the other person's desire to do well and please the family.

Anticipation

One of the most honorable methods of discipline is to anticipate potential problems and proactively respond to them. What times of the day, week, or month are most problematic for family members? Do they exhibit more behavior problems late at night, first thing in the morning, during the transition from school/work to home, or just before dinner? What activities present the opportunity for misbehavior related to boredom or anxiety?

Becoming aware of potential problem areas and times honors the other person by acknowledging and responding to their unique personality and needs. It also allows us to make plans that can avert difficulties, even turning a potential problem situation into an opportunity for growth.

John and his neurologist taught me this lesson of honor. John was a 6-year-old boy with a seizure disorder and hyperactivity. I used to take him and his family to various medical appointments, including his neurology appointments. Every appointment we attended was horrendous. John ran around the office getting into everything. As soon as we walked into a doctor's office he was opening the cupboard doors, jumping off the bed, looking in the sharps box, and playing with the stethoscope. Nothing was safe with John in the room. I dreaded going to appointments with him.

One day I took John to see his neurologist. As I chased him around the doctor's office trying to make him to sit down, his doctor walked in. I gave the doctor an exasperated shrug and he smiled. He knelt down and slowly wound up a small toy animal and set it on the ground. It barked and took a few steps before doing a flip and starting again. John loved it. He sat down and began to play while the doctor talked to his mother and me. I learned an important lesson about honor that day. From that time forward, I took several simple toys and activities to John's appointments. We would sit down together in the waiting room to play a game or make a craft while waiting for the doctor. Doctors' visits took on a whole new meaning. I no longer dreaded taking John to appointments but looked forward to the opportunity to talk with him about school and friends while we played simple games.

Conclusion

Honor and discipline go hand in hand for the intentional Christian family. In fact, intentional Christian families strive to honor one another in the midst of discipline. They do so by remembering that each family member is a work of art created in the image of God. In love, they attribute the best of intentions to one another and act on a belief that each family member ultimately wants to grow, especially when they have been raised in an atmosphere of honor and respect. With these beliefs firmly set, the family members honor one another in the speech that accompanies discipline. They anticipate future needs and prepare accordingly. In each of these ways, members of the intentional Christian family honor one another, even in the midst of discipline.

8 GOD'S HERITAGE OF GRACE

"For the grace of God has appeared, bringing salvation to all men, instructing us to deny ungodliness and worldly desires and to live sensibly, righteously and godly in the present age, looking for the blessed hope and the appearing of the glory of our great God and Savior, Christ Jesus, who gave Himself for us to redeem us from every lawless deed, and to purify for Himself a people for His own possession, zealous for good deeds."

Titus 2:11-14 (NASB)

"Christ came down from heaven, and whenever his disciples entertained dreams of prestige and power He reminded them that the greatest is the one who serves. The ladder of power reaches up, the ladder of grace reaches down."

–Philip Yancey

I began as a part-time youth minister in my early 20s. When I first arrived at the congregation I would serve, a family of four befriended me. As a young minister, this family presented me with several confusing dichotomies. They attended every worship service. Their two teenage boys actively participated in church activities and the youth group. In spite of their involvement, they never developed close relationships with other church members or even with each other. Instead, they seemed somewhat isolated. They welcomed me and befriended me, but I always felt as though they expected something in return.

The parents in this family maintained an extremely strict and structured home. Their teen boys had to pay rent to live in the house even though they were still in high school and also helped pay for groceries. They even paid for their own laundry detergent and soap. In spite of this excessive structure and active church involvement, the teens engaged in a great deal of misbehavior that included premarital sex, smoking, excessive swearing, and drinking. They also exhibited a sense of spiritual arrogance and moral superiority that left them unreceptive to the teaching of others in the Body of Christ.

The members of this family competed with one another for attention and admiration, even if it meant obtaining attention through comments that I considered caustic and hurtful. As time went on, I learned that they had judgmental and performance-based opinions of others. I discovered that their original kindness did, in fact, come with strings attached. When I did not agree with them, I experienced their rejection. When I said things they did not like, I fell out of their favor.

At the time, I found this family very confusing. Now, with more age and experience, I look back and realize what the problem was: They lacked grace. They had not experienced the full grace of God and, as a result, they could not share His grace with each other.

God did not design the graceless family. In fact, God designed the family to reflect Him. He created the family as one of the conduits of His grace. The intentional Christian family is a reflection of, and a training ground for, God's grace.

Grace, Uniquely Christian

Sin impacts all of us, Christian or not. I have sinned just as those who do not know Christ have sinned. And, like those who do not know Christ, I will sin again. One thing makes me very different from those who do not know Christ, however—the grace of God. God's grace alone brings me into relationship with Him, not my works or my "good behavior" (Ephesians 2:8-10). Only God's grace can turn the filthy rags of my sin into the pure white righteousness of Jesus Christ (Isaiah 1:18; Romans 3:21-22). By His grace, God has set me apart and made me His child, freeing me from death and sealing me with His Spirit (Ephesians 1:13-14) for an eternity in which I will experience the overwhelming love and kindness of God (Ephesians 2:4-7).

This concept of grace is the essential aspect of Christianity, the central theme of God's relationship with man. No other religion or belief system proclaims the unconditional, unmerited favor we find in Christ. Only Christianity gives us this heritage of grace.

The heritage of grace we have in Christ stands in stark contrast to the philosophies and practices of our society. Grace represents an unearned privilege, not a privilege or right we have earned. Grace is extravagantly generous, not frugal or limited. Grace, although extravagantly generous, carries no expectation of repayment, payment in kind, or a return favor. Grace offers a *no-strings-attached* policy.

Grace also provides the perfect balance between extravagant, generous, unconditional acceptance *and* loving discipline designed to promote growth. Titus 2:11-12 states that grace "instructs us." The Greek word translated "instructs" literally means "to train children" or "to chastise." Grace trains us as children of God to "deny ungodliness and worldly desires." Grace instructs us to "live sensibly, righteously, and godly." Grace that does not instruct us in such manners is no grace at all.

Stories of Grace

Jesus' stories are filled with characters who constantly show or receive God's grace. For example, the uninvited poor, crippled, blind, and lame became the invited guests at a king's banquet, even though they had no way to pay him back (Luke 14:12-24). The Good Samaritan revealed grace when he showed compassion and grace toward a person in need (Luke 10:25-37). A landowner generously paid his workers, whether they worked for one hour or a whole day (Matthew 20:1-16). A moneylender graciously forgave the debts of two people (Luke 7:41-43). Each of these stories reveal some aspect of God's heritage of grace.

The story of the prodigal son (Luke 15:11-32) tells the story of grace within the context of family. After the prodigal son had defied his father, squandered his inheritance on licentious living, and defamed the family name by becoming entwined in sinful living, his father graciously accepted him home. He forgave all wrongdoing, reinstated him in the family, and celebrated his return with the best he had to offer. The father showed so much grace to the prodigal son that his other son became jealous. Yes, Jesus' stories overflow with the virtue of grace and tell of the heritage of grace He offers.

Actions of Grace

Grace also flowed through Jesus' actions. Throughout His ministry, Jesus graciously reached out to the downcast, ignored, and rejected. He touched and healed the lepers, the blind, and the lame when no one else would touch them. He even touched a widow's dead son, giving him new life and then graciously giving him back to his mother (Luke 7:11-17).

Jesus exhibited grace when He called Matthew, a despised tax collector, to become one of His 12 disciples (Luke 5:29). He graciously allowed a woman known as a sinner within her community to wash His feet with her tears before anointing them with expensive perfume. Then, as the religious leaders complained about her extravagant and even "wasteful" (gracious) gift, He praised her for her love and forgave her (Luke 7:36-50). Jesus ate at Zacchaeus' house even though Zacchaeus was a self-confessed crooked tax collector and hated by the community in which he lived (Luke 19). He spoke with the woman at the well in spite of differences in gender, ethnicity, and level of morality and even made her His witness to the community in which her immorality was well-known (John 4:4-26). Jesus also protected and forgave the woman caught in adultery (John 8:1-8). The list of Jesus' gracious actions goes on and on…. He continually showed grace to the needy and rejected. His life overflowed with grace and He offered a heritage of grace to all He met.

The Ultimate Gift of Grace

Of course, Jesus' very purpose in coming to earth was to offer the gift of grace and provide a heritage of grace to all who would believe. Even when we were "dead in our transgressions" He showed us grace. When we were helpless, sinners, and enemies of God, Jesus Christ paid our debt of sin and brought us into the very presence of God, "raised us up with Him," "seated us with Him in heavenly places," and adopted us as His children, making us joint-heirs with Christ (Ephesians 2:4-10; Romans 5:6-11; Romans 8:14-17).

Ransomed by Grace

C.S. Lewis offers a beautiful allegory of God's ultimate gift of grace in *The Lion, The Witch and The Wardrobe*. In this story, Edmund betrays his brother and sisters to an evil witch in exchange for candy. Eventually, this betrayal led to his enslavement. Edmund found himself imprisoned by the witch and fearing for his life.

Meanwhile, his brother and sisters found Aslan the Lion and told him of Edmund's betrayal. That night, Aslan dispatched his army to rescue Edmund. They successfully raided the witch's camp and rescued Edmund. The next morning, Edmund's brother and sisters woke up to find Edmund home, safe and sound…at least for the moment.

The witch arrived at Aslan's camp the same morning and boldly demanded Edmund's life. She reminded Aslan that the law gave her every traitor as "lawful prey and that for every treachery I have a right to kill."

She claimed Edmund's life as "forfeit to [her]. His blood is my property." She went on to stake her claim on Edmund's life because "all Narnia will be overturned and perish in fire and water" if she did not spill his blood. Edmund's future looked bleak. The witch had every right to his life, and, without his life, the whole of Narnia would be destroyed.

If you have read the book, you know how it ends. Aslan gave himself in exchange for Edmund's life and freedom. He allowed the witch to humiliate and ridicule him instead of Edmund. In grace, he let the witch kill him rather than Edmund. Edmund's life was spared because Aslan gave his own life in exchange for Edmund's life.

In the same way, Jesus Christ gave Himself in exchange for us. Our life was forfeit to Satan because we had committed sin (Romans 3:23). We had betrayed Christ and belonged to Satan. By law, Satan demanded our life. He reminded Christ that "the wages of sin are death" (Romans 6:23). So Jesus Christ died for our sins, revealing to the world that "the free gift of God is eternal life" (Romans 6:23). Jesus, in obedience to His Father, exchanged His own life for our life so that we could be "justified as a gift by His grace through the redemption which is in Christ Jesus; whom God displayed publicly as a propitiation in His blood through faith" (Romans 3:24-25). Jesus wholeheartedly took our place, giving His own life to ransom our life from death (1 Timothy 2:5-6).

Redeemed by Grace

Aslan not only gave his life in exchange for Edmund's life but also gave Edmund back to his brother and sisters. As Aslan presented Edmund to his brother and sisters, he said, "Here is your brother and—there is no need to talk to him about what is past." There was no need to scold Edmund about his betrayal or to make him pay for his sin. Aslan planned to make that payment himself. He would redeem Edmund from the sin he had committed.

Jesus Christ does the same for us. He "gave Himself for us to redeem us from every lawless deed" (Titus 2:14). He set us free from our sins by making payment for the debt we incurred through our sin. The payment He made liberated us from our slavery to sin. He paid the price for our freedom. Jesus Christ paid the price to redeem us from those "lawless deeds" we committed with full knowledge and in ignorance. The Son of God Himself paid the price of our sins with His own life, not with perishable things such as gold or silver, but with His own imperishable blood. What an extravagant gift of grace!

Cleansed and Purified by Grace

Edmund became a better person after Aslan ransomed him from death and redeemed him from his sinful past. After his redemption, Edmund sacrificed himself in the final battle against the evil witch. He broke the witch's wand in an act that turned the tide of the battle. In the process, he was mortally wounded and lay dying on the battlefield. Fortunately, Lucy had received a gift of healing ointment. She quickly gave Edmund enough to restore his life. As Edmund returned to "his real old self," Aslan made him a knight. Throughout Narnia, he became known as King Edmund. On account of the gracious work of Aslan, Edmund had been transformed from a traitor to a kingly knight.

Jesus Christ gave Himself to make *us* better people as well. He gave Himself to cleanse us (Titus 2:14; Ephesians 5:25). The gift of grace in Jesus Christ purifies us; it washes away the guilt of our sin. Although as the old hymn puts it "sin had left a crimson stain; He washed it white as snow" in blood of the Lamb. When we stand before the judgment seat of God, He will not see our filthy, sin-stained lives. Instead, He will see His child, washed clean by the grace of God through the blood of Jesus Christ. He will see a child of the king, a fellow heir of Jesus Christ (Romans 8:17). By God's gracious work through Jesus Christ, we have been changed from sinful enemies to innocent children of God.

Sanctified by Grace

Jesus Christ gave Himself to sanctify us, to make us "holy and blameless" without "spot or wrinkle" (Ephesians 5:25-27). Grace makes us holy and separates us from the world. Accepting Christ's gift of grace by faith sets us apart and makes us worthy of God's recognition. Aslan recognized Edmund as a knight and a king. We Christians are recognized by God as the Church, the Bride of Christ. His grace makes it possible for Him to present His Church to Himself in "all her glory," as He had originally intended. Without this gift, we remain separated from God by sin, unrecognized by Him, and unworthy to come into His presence. Because of God's grace in Christ, He recognizes us as His children, the perfect Bride of Christ and welcomes us into His presence.

As I age, I look in the mirror to see my body changing—a few wrinkles and some grey hair (so I'm told). Physically, my body shows the wear-and-tear of aging. Spiritually, however, I look better everyday. In His grace, Christ continues to sanctify me and renew my spiritual body. Although "our outer man is decaying, our inward man is being renewed day by day, while we look not at those things which are seen but at those things which are unseen" (2 Corinthians 4:17-18). Every day we grow in God's grace and become a more perfect and beautiful bride for Christ.

Instructed by Grace

Jesus' gracious gift of Himself also instructs us in godly living. When someone invests himself in our lives, it changes us. We want to change because of the value he expresses through such an investment. Even more so, when Jesus Christ, the Creator and Sustainer of all things, invests Himself in our lives, we are compelled to change. This extravagant, generous gift of grace motivates us to "deny ungodliness and worldly desires" while pursuing a life that is "sensible, righteous, and godly" (Titus 2:12).

The grace of God revealed on the cross of Christ threw open the doors of heaven, tore down the barrier separating us from God, and united us with His family. We can do nothing to increase God's grace toward us and we can do nothing to diminish God's grace toward us. His grace is freely and abundantly given in extravagant measure. In no way can we earn or repay this grace. His grace, as revealed through Jesus Christ, is our assurance of salvation and it ignites our desire to live holy lives. What an amazing heritage of grace given through Jesus Christ!

Grace in God's Family

The heritage of grace we receive in Christ compels us to show mercy and grace to others. In the context of this book, God's heritage of grace compels us to show grace to our family members. If our families are to reflect Jesus Christ, we must make grace an integral part of our family. As we do so, our family will become a conduit of God's grace and a training ground for living in God's grace. And we will pass a heritage of grace to future generations.

Not all Christian families share God's heritage of grace with one another. Like the characters in Jesus' parable of the wedding feast (Matthew 22:1-14; Luke 16:16-24), some families become grace rejecters, others grace crushers, and still others grace manipulators. But, only the grace receivers in this parable enjoy the benefits of living within the heritage of God's grace. Consider each of the groups mentioned in this parable, beginning with grace rejecters.

Grace Rejecters

The grace rejecters refused the king's generous invitation to the feast. They simply ignored it, stating they had too much to do. Grace rejecters believe their own busy lives are more important than any invitation, no matter how gracious. Their focus on their own lives and everyday worries causes them to miss the significance of God's invitation. Trusting their own strength and provision, they have no time for a wedding or a feast. As a result, they refuse the invitation of grace.

Some families function as grace rejecters. Family members become so caught up in everyday activities and material possessions that they have no time to share God's grace with one another. Each person tries to build his own image in order to keep up with the neighbors. Image-conscious, they are too busy to accept God's extravagant gift of grace and too busy to practice grace towards one another.

Grace rejecters define themselves and others by their possessions and activities, and, ironically, they find themselves eventually enslaved by those very things. They reject the heritage of grace and find themselves struggling with personal insecurities and a poor self-image based on temporal possessions and fleeting achievements.

Grace Crushers

A second group of people in this parable crush the king's gift of grace. They actually "seized" those delivering the invitation and killed them. In their pride, rather than accepting the king's generous invitation of grace, they judged the king's servants as worthy of death. Their judgmental nature interfered with their ability to accept the gift of grace. This legalistic, judgmental spirit also prevented them from showing grace to the messenger. Rather than accept or show grace, they killed the messenger and thus crushed any prospect for receiving a gift of grace.

Families crush grace by legalistically focusing on the structure and rules of family life. Grace-crushing families act as though the rules will save them. They live by the motto "Follow the rules and all will turn out right and good." Family members are judged worthy of acceptance only as they perfectly adhere to an extensive set of rules and expectations. Achievement becomes mandatory. If family members fall short of the rules and expectations, they suffer rejection or punishment and, in some cases, are subject to being disowned or written off. Unfortunately, prioritizing rules and structure above family relationships only leads to a prideful, judgmental spirit within a family.

Grace crushers base worth on performance, and the quality of performance is fodder for comparisons among family members. As a result, grace-crushing families make comparisons among family members: "Why can't you be like Johnny in school?" or "If only you had Susan's athletic gifts...." They also compare family members to those outside the family: "Why can't you be the kind of husband Joe is?" or "I'm sure glad we're not like the...." These performance-based comparisons and judgments can lead to despair or arrogance. There is always someone who will eventually perform better, however. When this "superior" person comes along, arrogance turns to shame, anger, resentment, and insecurity. Family members may over-compensate for the resulting insecurity by becoming overly competitive.

Legalism within the family also encourages hypocrisy. Members of a legalistic family *appear* as though they live up to expectations. Externally, they look like the picture-perfect family. Like the family I described at the beginning of this chapter, they attend church regularly and appear actively involved. Beneath this shallow façade, however, lies an excessive competition for acceptance, a fear-based obedience that harbors resentment, and a lack of self-control that leads to rebellion when the external controls are removed.

Grace Manipulators

A third group of characters in Jesus' parable accepted the king's invitation on their own terms. They arrived at the wedding feast wearing their own clothes rather than the clothes provided by the host. They came to the wedding dressed in their own works and effort. They hoped that their new relationship with the king would enable them to continue wearing the same old clothes. The grace manipulators believed in a lazy grace that would allow them to continue living the same old life. They wanted to manipulate the king's graciousness to receive the benefits of his invitation without making any changes. The king threw them out of the reception, however. He had not offered a lazy grace, but an instructive grace that would teach them to "live sensibly, righteously, and godly" (Titus 2:11-14).

Families of grace manipulators practice lazy grace. They focus on relationships, believing that simply accepting one another will lead to appropriate interactions and behaviors. Grace manipulators act as though a strong relationship erases the need for instructive discipline.

I met a woman whose 6-year-old son would literally beat on her when he became angry. When I asked her why she allowed this type of abusive behavior, she explained: "I love him and he needs to get that anger out. Better he do it to me than someone else. He'll outgrow it." The bad news is that he will not outgrow it unless he learns true grace. He will continue to experience difficulty controlling his emotions until he receives the instructive discipline of grace. In fact, he may actually grow resentful and run wild in search of some kind of boundary to show him how to "live sensibly, righteously and godly." True grace "instructs us in denying ungodliness and worldly desires and to live sensibly, righteously and godly in the present age" (Titus 2:11-12).

I attended a college in the early 1980s that had a strict dress code. According to the dress code, I was to wear a tie to supper and a jacket and tie to chapel. I remember wearing my tie—*loosely*—around my neck. I had a jacket but carried it on my arm rather than wearing it appropriately. I practiced a lazy grace while looking for a loophole. I tried to manipulate the system while expecting my "membership" in college to protect me from the discipline I deserved for continuing to dress "in the same old way."

Grace does not accept this type of behavior. A heritage of grace provides instruction in right and sensible living—the type of living that will bring us the greatest joy and success.

Grace Receivers

A final group of people did accept the king's invitation on the *king's* terms. They arrived wearing the clothes the king provided and enjoyed the wedding feast. They accepted God's grace and changed in response to His grace. They willingly became a part of God's heritage of grace.

Families that become a part of God's heritage of grace provide strong relationships and loving structure because they provide *both* grace *and* truth. They know that true grace provides the loving relationships that build each person up and affirm each person's sense of significance and purpose as well as the boundaries that teach gracious living and produce long-term security. True grace enhances each person's ability to appropriately and lovingly manage conflict and the emotions that accompany conflict.

A heritage of grace allows for mutual unselfishness. Said another way: Grace allows for extravagant generosity to one another rather than always seeking "what's in it for me." Grace provides the love and limits that give people the strength and freedom to give themselves wholeheartedly to the family. Grace allows family members to struggle with vulnerabilities within the security of an unconditionally loving family. It allows family members to practice honesty, knowing the joy of complete acceptance in spite of mistakes. And grace provides complete acceptance in the midst of loving discipline.

Manager at the House of Grace

God calls us to minister to one another as good stewards of His grace (1 Peter 4:10) to continue the heritage of grace He began. Although Peter wrote this in relation to the Church, I believe it applies equally well to the family. We need to act as stewards of God's grace within the family, helping to establish a household of grace. We do so by sharing the grace God has given us with our family members. Individually, we are what Yancey (1997) refers to as a grace dispenser, generously dispensing God's grace to each person within our family. Join me now as we set the stage for God's heritage of grace in our family.

9 SETTING THE STAGE

"Feeling accepted for just being themselves creates a secure feeling that no matter what happens, they'll be loved. That kind of accepting relationship creates a loving bond and an intimate relationship."

–Josh McDowell

Christ amazes me. He lived a perfectly holy life. Yet in spite of His perfect righteousness, sinners loved Him. They sought out His company and crowded around Him. Jesus had so many sinners around Him that His detractors called Him a "friend of sinners" (Matthew 11:19). In fact, He did befriend sinners. He accepted hotheads like Peter, James, and John into His inner circle of friends. He also accepted a tax collector like Matthew, even though tax collectors were despised. Jesus even went to a party at Matthew's house where He mingled with a whole house full of "tax collectors and sinners" (Matthew 2:15-17). Jesus accepted each of these people, and His acceptance brought change into their lives.

Children enjoyed being with Jesus, too. They were drawn to Him. At one point the disciples tried to chase them away, but Jesus told the disciples to let the children come to Him. Jesus wanted the children to come to Him. He accepted the children. He even said we must become like children to enter into His kingdom (Matthew 19:13-14).

Jesus never rejected anyone who truly sought Him out—whether a sinner, a Pharisee, a child, a rich man of influence, or a blind beggar. Jesus accepted them all. In turn, Paul tells Christians to "accept one another, just as Christ also accepted us to the glory of God" (Romans 15:7). The Greek word translated "accept" literally means "to receive into one's home with the purpose of showing kindness; to take into a friendship and granting access to one's heart; to take by the hand to lead aside." Acceptance, then, implies developing a heart-felt relationship with another person from which we can show them kindness. This type of grace-motivated acceptance sets the stage for the giving and sacrifice of grace.

God calls us to imitate the model of acceptance Jesus set for us and that is recorded in Scripture. But what does that acceptance look like? How did Jesus Christ accept us? After all, if we are to "accept one another, just as Christ accepted you to the glory of God" we have to know how Christ accepted us.

While We Were Helpless

Christ accepted us while we were still helpless (Romans 5:6). Jesus modeled this type of acceptance when He met the Samaritan woman at the well (John 4). From our multi-cultural perspective, we don't find anything particularly extraordinary about Jesus' talking with a Samaritan woman. In the world and time of Jesus, however, this was an extraordinary act of gracious acceptance. In Jesus' time and culture men did not speak with women. In addition, Jews did not associate with Samaritans. Yet here we find Jesus, a respected Jewish man and teacher (rabbi), graciously talking to this Samaritan woman of dubious reputation. He befriended her and accepted her into His heart. Jesus received her with the intent of showing kindness, not just to her but to her whole community. He accepted her in spite of her gender and ethnicity, both of which she was helpless to change.

While We Were Sinners

He accepted us while we were sinners (Romans 5:8). Jesus modeled this acceptance for us when the Pharisees brought an adulterous woman to Him for judgment (John 8:1-11). Jesus did not pass judgment on the woman, despite the fact that she had committed a capital offense punishable by stoning. Instead, He knelt down and wrote on the ground. Although we do not know what Jesus wrote, all those who condemned the adulterous woman left as they read what He wrote. Eventually, only Jesus and the woman remained. Jesus then asked the woman who was left there to condemn her. The woman looked at Jesus and replied, "No one, Lord." Jesus confirmed her perception by saying, "I do not condemn you, either."

Jesus accepted this woman in spite of her sin and moral failings. He took her in with the intent of showing her kindness; but He did not leave her in her sin. Instead, He "took her aside" and, with His final words to her, admonished her to "sin no more." Note, however, that His call to change was issued only after He had affirmed His acceptance of the woman. Jesus' first act of grace was to accept her not to judge her. He took her in, showed her kindness, and assured her that He accepted her. *Then* He called her to change.

Jesus was so accepting of sinners, in fact, that the Pharisees complained about Him "eating and drinking with sinners" (Matthew 9:11). Jesus knew about these accusations. Once while speaking to a crowd, Jesus noted that people called Him a "gluttonous man and a drunkard, a friend of tax collectors and sinners" (Matthew 11:19). Knowing what others said did not stop Him from accepting sinners. He continued to graciously accept people, even in their sin, while holding out a standard of perfect holiness.

While We Were Enemies

Jesus also accepted *us* while our sins made us His enemies (Romans 5:10). Jesus modeled this level of acceptance during the last supper (John 13). Jesus knew that His time to die was fast approaching. In order to teach His disciples a final lesson, He assumed a servant's role and washed their feet. After washing the disciples' feet, Jesus sat at the table with the disciples and began to share a meal. He told them that someone would betray Him. They began to ask who would do such a thing. Jesus said, "The one for whom I shall dip the morsel and give it to him." Jesus then dipped the bread and gave it to Judas. As he did, He told Judas, "What you do, do quickly."

Jesus knew that Judas would betray Him. He knew this "from the beginning" (John 6:64), yet He accepted Judas, humbly washed His feet, and graciously shared His final meal with him. He accepted Judas—His betrayer, His enemy. Jesus received Judas into His supper and showed Him kindness. He offered Judas His hand in friendship.

Unconditional Acceptance in the Family

If we want to reflect the grace of God within our families, we must set the stage by graciously accepting each family member as Christ accepts us— *unconditionally*. Acceptance actually satisfies a deep-seated emotional need in each of us. Markman (1994) calls acceptance the "mother of all issues." He explains how issues of power, commitment, recognition, and caring all stem from one or both people in a relationship feeling a lack of acceptance.

Lack of acceptance feels like rejection or abandonment, which people perceive as a threat to their well-being. In fact, rejection by a loved one does threaten our emotional and physical health. Rejection increases the stress hormones in our body, decreases our coping skills, and even hinders our immune functioning (Johnson, 2009). In response to feeling rejected, we strive to regain a sense of acceptance. Like a toddler crying out and reaching for her mother, we strive for acceptance by acting out our fear of rejection. We become so overwhelmed with the fear of rejection and our efforts to regain acceptance that we have no energy to invest in change. In other words, a lack of acceptance hinders change and retards emotional growth.

Unconditional acceptance, on the other hand, gives us a sense of security. It builds an awareness that we are loved in spite of our mistakes and failings. Unconditional acceptance gives us a sense of confidence. It allows us to "step out" and try new things, confident that even if we fail we will be supported not rejected. Unconditional acceptance opens the door to change and even encourages growth. It empowers us to face difficult times with courage. When all is said and done, acceptance makes our family home the greatest place on Earth.

To summarize, unconditional acceptance meets a basic, deep-seated need within each one of us. It promotes a sense of security, confidence, and courage. Grace-motivated acceptance "frees up" the energy that we would invest in protesting perceived rejection so that we can invest that energy in growth. When given in grace, acceptance sets the stage for a grace-filled family.

The Tension

Grace-motivated acceptance modeled on Christ's acceptance is the exact opposite of the world's idea of acceptance. Our society does not accept people unconditionally. Instead, society encourages acceptance based on performance, achievement, and ability. We hear statements encouraging people to "pull themselves up by their bootstraps," "work hard to make something of yourself," and "I'll respect them when they earn it." Acceptance is conditional in our world, a privilege to be earned, rather than the grace-motivated act of love we want to incorporate into our families.

This performance-based, achievement-oriented mentality sneaks into the family in subtle and not-so-subtle ways. For instance, we might show greater love and acceptance to the family member who takes the limelight by way of a strong personality or some special ability. Perhaps, without realizing it, we show honor and affection when family members behave in a manner consistent with our expectations or silent demands and ignore them when they simply act like themselves.

Conditional acceptance also sneaks into family relationships in the form of back-handed compliments such as "You did a good job...for a change" or conditional praises such as telling a child "I love you so much" only when she behaves in certain ways *we* like. Such compliments and ill-timed praises imply that love and acceptance are only available when a person meets certain conditions or lives up to specific expectations. They communicate a subtle message that if a person does not meet those conditions, he or she will not be granted access into the family heart.

Grace-crushing families may go a step further, adding guilt and shame to the arsenal of weapons they use to evoke compliance and earn acceptance. In such families, if a person does not perform or behave in an acceptable manner, the family uses guilt and shame to prod and cajole them into behaving within expectations.

Read the following statements and think about how they show conditional acceptance.

Statement	How it shows conditional acceptance
"That's a nice job, *for you.*"	*Back-handed compliment* implies that person cannot or does not meet the acceptable standard most of the time.
"Good work, *for a change.*"	*Back-handed compliment* implies that the person does not usually do an acceptable job.
"You can't do anything right, can you?"	A *criticism* implying the person is incapable and therefore unacceptable.
"Be a good boy (girl) and carry my plate in."	A *conditional statement* implying a person must behave in a certain way to receive acceptance and to "be good."
"Why can't you be like your cousin?"	A *comparison* implies that the "other person is good enough, not me. I'm not acceptable unless I am like someone else."
"Her husband is so good-looking and strong, but he still brings home flowers. You never bring me flowers."	Once again, a *comparison* implying that "I'm not acceptable unless I am like someone else."
"If you really loved me, you would_____."	*Guilt-inducing* statement implying "I'm only acceptable when I carry out the request."
"After all I've done for you, how could you do that to me?"	*Guilt-inducing* statement implying "I'm not acceptable because I displeased another person."

These statements and the performance-oriented mindset behind them tear down the house of grace a brick at a time. Grace is unconditional; legalism is totally conditional. The intentional Christian family is grace-full not legalistic. Grace-full families avoid such performance-based statements which, whether implicitly or explicitly, point to conditional acceptance based on legalistic standards. The person on the receiving end of such statements experiences rejection, and feeling rejected hinders growth and change. In fact, feeling rejected leads to poor self-image, a crushing sense of guilt and shame, and more fear-based behavior aimed at finding unconditional acceptance.

God, on the other hand, calls us to accept one another as Jesus Christ accepted us. Jesus Christ accepted us in grace. He gave us the gracious gift of unconditional acceptance based on the inherent worth with which He created us. Building a heritage of grace within our families calls us to accept one another for who we are, human beings created in the image of God.

Even When Helpless

Families building a heritage of grace follow Jesus' example in accepting one another in spite of our helplessness. There are at least three areas in which family members are "helpless": developmental abilities, interests, and temperament.

Family members naturally have different developmental abilities. Abilities also change as people mature and age. I recall sitting with my wife at a restaurant near a young family of three. The mom and dad were trying to make their 2½-3-year-old son sit still and eat. He was eating, mind you, but he was fidgety. He would take a bite or two and then begin talking. He had a lot to say. He pointed this way and that, shuffled his legs, shifted in his seat. Then he would take a few more bites and repeat the process. Although he was eating, his parents were becoming frustrated. They wanted him to "sit still" and "stop fidgeting." When he did not stop, they resorted to threats. They told him that they were going to "take his stuffed bear away" and "never take him out again." Over the course of their meal, they became increasingly frustrated and harsh until finally they left with a sobbing toddler in tow.

This toddler was acting like a toddler. He was helpless to act any other way. In fact, his behavior was just fine and developmentally appropriate. He was not too loud. He was eating. And he was fidgety and talkative, like a healthy toddler. He needed his family to accept him despite his developmental needs and to accept him as he was.

Younger children often try to imitate their "big brother" or "big sister." They try and try but become frustrated because they have not yet developed the coordination, strength, or skill that their older siblings have already developed. Sometimes, I hear family members compare a younger sibling to an older one and yell at the younger member based on these developmental differences. The younger child is helpless in this area. He cannot control his own development. Instead of comparing and pushing, a grace-filled family will accept those different developmental abilities and encourage the children themselves not to compare any member with another. The grace-filled family will receive each child and adult into the family's heart in order to show him kindness and encouragement at whatever developmental level he has achieved.

Family members often have different talents and interests as well. For instance, some family members may demonstrate musical or artistic talent while others might have an aptitude for math. Families building a heritage of grace will accept each person and her particular ability. Though this may sound obvious, families do not always do this. I met a family whose father was very interested in sports. His life had revolved around basketball and football when he was in high school. As an adult, he involved himself in various community sporting leagues for adults. His son, however, enjoyed reading books and writing. He enjoyed playing music with his friends. His father had a very difficult time accepting his son and his very different interests. "He should be out there playing football, not inside playing a guitar with his friends. What kind of friends are they anyway?"

Family members will rarely all have the same (or even similar) talents and interests. Most likely they do not try to cultivate different interests—it just happens. Enjoy those differences. Celebrate them as opportunities to share and grow. Learn a little bit about other members' interests and appreciate what they do to become accomplished in that area. Above all, accept their talents and interests as a legitimate expression of who they are as persons created by God and endowed with certain gifts.

In many ways, a person's temperament is beyond his control. Although we can influence our temperament to some degree, we seem to fall within a certain range no matter how hard we try. For instance, some people are naturally happy all the time, others tend toward melancholy. Some people are shy, others are outgoing. Some people like to play then work whereas others like to work then play. Some people are very expressive; others are rather quiet and less expressive. Some people show emotions easily while others seem to focus instead on calm explanations. You get the point: People have different personalities. Families building a heritage of grace will accept one another in spite of their temperamental differences.

When They Miss the Mark

Families that build a heritage of grace will also follow Jesus' example in accepting family members who miss the mark. We have to face the facts: Everybody makes mistakes, even family members. Children misbehave. Teens show attitude. Adolescents forget to do their chores. Spouses engage in rude or thoughtless behavior. Parents make mistakes. Parents may even misunderstand their child's behavior and make a poor decision from time to time. We *all* "miss the mark."

Sometimes families become so angry about someone "missing the mark" that they reject the wrongdoer. They may reject the person who "missed the mark" by ignoring him, threatening to leave him, or expressing remorse about even being a part of the family. Too many times I have heard a parent yell "I wish you had never been born" or "You ruined my life" in the midst of anger over some misbehavior. How devastating to a child—to hear his own parent tell him that he has ruined the life of the person he looks up to and admires.

Such exchanges occur between other family members as well. For instance, the spouse who yells "I wish I'd never married you" in the midst of an argument or the child who yells "You're so embarrassing, I hate you" at her parent is rejecting that family member because he "missed the mark." These interactions cause fractures in the relationship by communicating rejection and conditional love and acceptance.

Interestingly, Jesus even accepted people who "missed the mark." In fact, He seemed to seek out those who had "missed the mark." He came to "heal the sick, not the healthy" and "to seek and to save those who were lost." He knew that those who missed the mark had a deep need to feel connected and accepted. Such people need to be taken by the hand, given access into our heart, and shown kindness. Only from the basis of a loving and accepting relationship could Jesus show them how to live the abundant life.

Families building a heritage of grace follow Christ's example. They work to accept one another even when someone misses the mark. They may discipline inappropriate behavior and even express anger but only within the boundaries of an obvious loving and accepting relationship. Experience over time assures each family member that she is accepted beyond a shadow of a doubt. All family members know that they have access to one another's heart. They know they are accepted even in the midst of conflict and discipline.

When Feeling Betrayed

Families are a great source of joy…most of the time. On the other hand, no one can hurt us like the ones we love. Family members know us intimately, and this intimacy leaves us vulnerable to pain. Pain inflicted by family members, either accidentally or purposefully, seems to hurt so much more than that caused by strangers. Sometimes it feels like a betrayal. We feel as though the one to whom we have given our life has betrayed our love. They have taken the precious gift of our life and abused it. A child who defames the family name by getting drunk at a party…a parent who loses control and strikes his child…a spouse who falls into an emotional or physical affair…harsh statements made in the heat of anger…or simply not "being there" to comfort a family member at a key moment…each of these can inflict a deep wound that causes lasting damage to a relationship. Sometimes the harmful behavior is as obvious as an affair or a slanderous statement. Other times, the harmful behavior is only obvious to the one who was hurt.

Joe knew his wife was emotionally upset. But she said she was all right. They had talked about how her best friend had abandoned her in response to a misunderstanding. He had offered a good solution. His wife was still upset, but since she told him that she was all right, he went on a night out with the guys. He thought everything was fine until the next day when, during a small disagreement, she screamed, "You're never there for me!" As they talked, he discovered that she had felt abandoned when he left her to go out with the guys the previous night. He had not realized the pain she felt. Unfortunately, she felt betrayed, abandoned, and all alone. Joe and his wife had a good relationship and quickly resolved this incident. It shows, however, that sometimes we hurt our family members without even realizing it.

Whether the hurtful behavior is obvious or not, the resulting damage often requires an apology and forgiveness to completely resolve. Moving toward forgiveness and reconciliation requires an attitude of acceptance and a willingness to receive the other person into the space of our life with the intention of showing kindness to her. Families that build a heritage of grace have practiced this acceptance. They have taken one another by the hand, given access into their hearts, and shown kindness over time. At times of hurt, they have a foundation of acceptance in place. They can build on this foundation to strengthen their heritage of grace. (Forgiveness will be discussed in greater detail in Chapter 12.)

Setting the Stage

Acceptance involves coming alongside of one another, granting access to our hearts, and showing kindness to one another just as Christ did for us. Such grace-motivated acceptance sets the stage for giving ourselves to our family, making sacrifices for our family, and forgiving one another as the need arises.

10 GRACE BEGINS

. . . .

"The ability to attend to our partner's deeper disclosures is the beginning of mutual responsiveness and engagement."

— Sue Johnson

"Good fathering implies a willingness to give up some of our self-centeredness. Good fathering requires the defeat of some of our overbearing narcissism. When you are being a good father you love another unselfishly, without ulterior motive."

—Aaron Hass

John 3:16 tells us that "God so loved the world…"—a sinful world that He graciously chose to accept. In order to grant that world eternal access to His heart and to show her the unlimited kindness of His love "He gave…." "God so loved the world that He gave" not just *any* gift, but the unprecedented and undeserved gift of "His only begotten Son." And so with the precious gift of Himself grace begins.

Acceptance may set the stage, but grace begins with *giving.* It begins as an extravagant and generous gift given with no strings attached and no ulterior motive, a gift given with full knowledge that the person cannot pay it back. God's gift of Jesus Christ and Jesus Christ's willing gift of Himself exemplifies this grace. What greater gift can we give than the gift of our self? Yes, grace begins when we, like Christ, give of our self for the benefit of the other.

A Gracious Gift of Self

Jesus Christ gave Himself to us and accomplished His work of grace by dying on the cross for us. I don't know about you, but I hope I never have to die on a cross for my family. So how can I show grace to my family? How do I apply this concept of grace—which is so essential to Christianity—to my family life?

Remember, grace begins with giving and includes giving of the self for the benefit of others. To show grace within the family, we begin by giving the gift of ourselves. The gift of our self involves putting aside our own agenda and committing our lives to our family members in order to benefit them. The gift of self is measured by availability, attentiveness, and emotional connectedness. In a sense, these three factors—availability, attentiveness, and emotional connectedness—become the currency with which our family measures the value of our gift. Let's explore each of these measures individually.

The Gift of Availability

God has been available to His people since the beginning of creation. He walked with Adam and Eve in the garden. He talked with Abraham to call him into the Promise Land. He saw the tears of the Israelites as they worked as slaves in Egypt and delivered them from Egyptian bondage. God remained available as He led them through the wilderness with His presence.

God's availability continued in the New Testament with the birth of Jesus Christ—Emmanuel: "God with us." Jesus became a man and walked among us. He was available to His disciples throughout His ministry. Whenever someone sought Jesus, He made Himself available to him or her. When the disciples tried to shoo the children away, Jesus said, "Let the little children come unto Me" (Mark 10:14). He was available to them. When the people tried to shoo the blind man away, Jesus stopped and asked the blind man a question (Mark 10:47-52). When the people tried to keep Zacchaeus away, Jesus went to his house for dinner (Luke 19:2-7). In spite of an amazingly busy schedule, Jesus always seemed available to speak to anyone who genuinely wanted to speak with Him.

Jesus remains available to us as well. After He ascended into Heaven, He poured out His Holy Spirit to dwell in us (Acts 2). As Christians, we now have the indwelling Holy Spirit—Christ in us, our hope of glory (Colossians 1:27). He is constantly present in our lives—empowering us, guiding us, and instructing us.

> "He walks with me, and He talks with Me
> And He tells me I am His own;
> And the joy we share as we tarry there
> None other has ever known." (Miles, *In the Garden*)

Jesus Christ, the One who sustains all things and holds all things together, takes time to "tarry" with us. He remains available enough to continue with us in prayer, to kick back and converse with us. What a beautiful thought.

Becoming Available

Josh McDowell (2000) says that people spell love "T-I-M-E." Becoming available to our families requires that we make time for them, that we "tarry" with them. People often get so caught up in their busy schedules that they lose the time necessary to remain available to their family. To build a heritage of grace in our family, however, requires that we "tarry there."

"Yeah, but it's the *quality* time I spend with family that's important." Quality time is important. But the idea that quality time makes up for quantity is a myth; it is just not true. We cannot separate quality from quantity when it comes to time. In fact, quality time demands a quantity of time. It is only when we spend a quantity of time together that we find those moments of quality. Quality time occurs spontaneously in the midst of quantity time.

Imagine I were to offer you one of two gifts. Option 1 is a nice, crisp $5 bill, freshly minted and of great quality. Option 2 is 25 old, wrinkled, crumpled up, and creased $1 bills. Which would you prefer—the quality $5 bill or the quantity of 25 $1 bills? Most of us would choose the quantity over quality (I tried to talk my 11-year-old daughter into the quality $5 bill, but she wouldn't go for it). For some reason, we seem to think about our time with family differently. We assume that our family desires only quality time (a crisp, new $5 bill), not quantity time (25 old, wrinkled $1 bills). Families of grace, on the other hand, share both quantity time and quality time. They discover that they create the opportunities to experience quality time by spending a quantity of time together.

The Gracious Gift of Attentiveness

Availability represents one way in which family members measure our gift of self. Attentiveness represents another. We are drawn to those who show genuine interest in us and pay attention to us.

I believe this is one of the reasons people loved Jesus so much. He gave His full attention to those with whom He interacted. His attentiveness revealed a deep value and love for the people with whom He spoke. The woman at the well, the woman caught in adultery, the lepers, Nicodemus… they all must have felt deeply valued as they spoke to Jesus and became recipients of His attentive love.

Mike, an elementary-school-age child, taught me the importance of attentiveness in relationships. He desperately wanted his mother's attention, but she seemed more interested in the TV. When he approached her calmly, she gave one-word responses and never took her eyes off the TV. She paid him very little attention and gave the impression that her relationship with the TV was more important to her than her relationship with Mike.

What do you think Mike did? He became increasingly energetic in his demand for attention. He grew louder and more active in his demands until his mother had no choice but to turn her attention to him. In anger, she turned to Mike and began screaming at him. Finally, he had her attention. He had more of a connection with her than she had with the TV. It was an unpleasant connection, to be sure, but an attentive connection nonetheless.

Over time, Mike learned to bypass calm attempts to gain attention from his mother and immediately engaged in those behaviors that led to his mother's energetic, albeit angry, interaction with him. Her attention—even negative attention—was reward enough. In other words, he learned to "act up" in order to gain his mother's energetic attention. He valued her attention so much that he did "whatever it took" to get it.

Adults also measure the gift of self in terms of attention. When we believe that our partner invests less attention in our relationship than in some other relationship or pursuit, we feel threatened and scared. We then attempt to regain our partner's attentive involvement with us. Ideally, we approach our partner by openly communicating our concerns and he or she reciprocates with genuine attentiveness to our feelings and needs. Many couples, however, react by protesting the loss of attention in ways that seem counterproductive, such as fighting, blaming, or withdrawing. Whatever the behavior, the person is crying out for genuine attentive interest from the other person.

Whether children or adults, we all want to know that our family members value us enough to attentively engage in an intimate relationship with us. As attentiveness is freely invested, intimacy grows.

Distracted Attention

Simple interactions throughout the day reveal our level of attentiveness to family members. For instance, Mike's mother was preoccupied with her favorite activity (watching TV) and invested all her attention in that activity. She invested little attention in Mike. Simple one-word answers, a distant smile, and no eye contact revealed that she had very little desire to attend to Mike or her relationship with him.

As I was waiting in line for the roller coaster during a trip to a local amusement park this summer, I watched a mother and son finish the ride. The mother carefully stepped off of the roller coaster while reading and sending text messages on her phone. The son silently followed her. Even on the roller coaster, this mother's attention was elsewhere—on whomever she was texting! She was *with* him in body, but she was not attentive to him.

I have a friend who engages in similar behavior. When we stand in line for a ride or drive to a movie, he constantly checks his phone for the headlines or responds to e-mails. He is with me, but he is not attentive. This lack of attentiveness prevents our relationship from growing by limiting the opportunities we have for intimate sharing.

You may have responded with this level of attentiveness yourself. Perhaps you were too tired or preoccupied with some project so you faked attention. I know I have; we have all done it from time to time. When this level of attentiveness becomes habitual, or typical, however, our family suffers. The gift of self becomes limited and intimacy is lost.

Selfish Attention

Mike's mother could have given Mike just enough attention to pick out some insignificant detail of what He said and use that to get him "out of her hair." Or she might have interrupted him in order to change the topic back to the TV show she was watching. Either of these responses would still have revealed less attentiveness to Mike than to her personal interests.

People who do this regularly attend more to their selfish interests than to relational interests and the interests of their family members and friends. They selfishly communicate a lack of interest in the other person and the belief that the other person is not as valuable as other things in their life. They do not give themselves to the relationship.

Genuine Attention

Mike's mother could have responded with full sentences and simple gestures to show more attentiveness. This type of attentiveness shows more interest in the person and encourages further interaction. She could have expanded her verbal responses enough to engage Mike in a full conversation to become even more attentive. She could share her opinions, thoughts, and feelings with Mike to deepen her attentiveness and engage with him at more intimate level. This level of attentiveness reveals a deeper giving of our self and places a greater value on the relationship to the other person than on whatever other activity we might engage in (such as watching TV).

The more attentive we remain during interactions, the more we give of ourselves. The more we give of ourselves, the more we communicate a genuine interest in the other person. The other person experiences our attentiveness as validation of his worth and value in our eyes. He will also know that we desire and pursue a deeper relationship with him. When another person responds more attentively to us and seeks us out more often, intimacy deepens. When family members give the gift of attention, the whole family begins to experience God's heritage of grace.

The Gift of Emotional Connectedness

Emotions provide a fertile ground on which to connect and build intimacy. They reveal our deepest priorities, our greatest fears, and our most fervent needs. As we share our emotions with one another, our burdens become lighter and our intimacy deepens. Perhaps that is one of the reasons that Scripture commands us to "rejoice with those who rejoice and weep with those who weep" (Romans 12:15).

Sharing emotions demands our availability and attentiveness and leads to emotional connectedness, a deeper giving of the self. Emotional connectedness allows us to become open and transparent with our feelings, meeting one another in areas of vulnerability as well as areas of strength. Emotionally connected families remain available and attentive to one another in the angry and depressing emotional valleys as well as the ecstatic, joyous emotional mountain tops. They use each and every experience as an opportunity to grow more intimate and secure with one another.

Emotional connectedness has many benefits for family members. Children who have a strong emotional connection to their family are more affectionate with their parents. They get along with other people better and show more social skill. Not surprisingly, they also tend to be more popular with peers. In addition, they exhibit fewer behavior problems and can calm themselves when upset. They pay attention better and learn more efficiently and, as a result, have higher achievement scores (Johnson, 2008).

Adults with a strong emotional connection to family exhibit less anger and remain more open to new information. They like themselves better and more readily seek out support from others. They also offer support to others more readily. Similarly, adults with a strong emotional connection have the strength and resources necessary to behave more independently. They have healthier immune systems. In fact, at least one researcher suggests that emotional isolation may be a more dangerous risk factor than smoking or high blood pressure (Johnson, 2008). Overall, emotional connectedness improves our physical, social, and cognitive health. Emotional connectedness helps create a heritage of grace.

Too Cold...Too Hard

If Goldilocks would have observed the emotional connection in the home of the three bears, she may have witnessed one kind that was "too cold and too hard." In this type of emotional connection, family members learn to have disdain for emotions. Emotions are considered a sign of weakness or an attempt to manipulate others. Family members grow ashamed of emotions. As a result, they forbid the display of emotions. They may even criticize or punish the expression of negative emotion. The person experiencing emotions may feel that others are judging him as he hears comments such as "Quit crying or I'll give you something to cry about" or "Quit crying...you're only embarrassing yourself."

A little less extreme are the families that simply ignore emotions. These families consider emotions a nuisance or a bother. They are uncomfortable with emotions and do their best to pretend they don't exist—especially the negative ones. In addition, family members focus on getting over the emotion instead of finding and resolving the potential meaning behind the emotion.

Unfortunately, both of these approaches withhold the gift of emotional connectedness and hinder grace. In avoiding emotional connectedness, these families teach that feelings are wrong. Family members who have feelings—which we all do—come to believe that they have a flaw because of their emotions. This belief contributes to lower self-esteem. In addition, children do not learn how to deal with emotions and, as a result, become more argumentative, conflictual, withdrawn, or mopey. Stifled emotions will be expressed either positively or negatively...but they *will* be expressed.

Too Small...Too Soft

At the other end of the continuum, Goldilocks might have found an emotional connectedness that was "too small and too soft." In this family, people are permissive with emotions. They practice a lazy grace—a grace without instruction. Family members give of themselves emotionally but offer no instruction on how to appropriately manage emotions. Such families accept the emotion and whatever behavior comes with it. They offer no constraints on behaviors that might accompany emotions. Anger or frustration that is expressed in yelling, screaming, and even physical aggression is simply accepted with the blithe "that's just the way he feels." No limits are set. Sadness that is expressed in days-long withdrawal from the family, school, and other responsibilities is not confronted but accepted as a "natural" response. The resounding mantra is: "It's OK, just let it out."

This style of emotional connectedness lacks grace as well as its counterpart, emotional denial and disconnectedness. Family members in such a family become overwhelmed with powerful emotions because they don't know how to manage them. They have trouble concentrating as emotions intrude into their lives. And, as you can imagine, they often have trouble forming long-term, intimate relationships because volatile emotions that erupt in "blow ups" and "shut downs" push others away.

Overall, both of these extremes limit a family's emotional connection. Family members either feel flawed for having emotions or overwhelmed by not being able to effectively manage their emotions. They have great difficulty expressing the normal emotions they experience and find it difficult even to concentrate at times. Because they have never learned strategies for effectively managing their emotions, family members are likely to blow up in response to strong emotions. These flare-ups of emotion interfere with intimacy among family members. Overall, lacking the emotional connection that comes with the heritage of grace contributes to distant relationships, increased conflict, and poor self-esteem among family members.

Just Right

Goldilocks would find in the grace-filled family an emotional connectedness that was "just right." With a "just right" emotional connection, family members recognize emotions as they occur and value them as opportunities to build intimacy. At the same time, they place appropriate limits on the behavioral expression of emotion and teach effective ways to manage emotions rather than being managed by them. They give of themselves emotionally, teaching and learning to express emotions through conversation, tears, laughter, hugs, and holding. They rejoice with one another and weep with one another. They learn to call emotions by name. As a result, they also learn to express and act on their feelings in a positive manner. As a family, they use emotions as a starting point to learn more about one another, to grow more intimate with one another, and to solve problems within the Christian boundaries of grace. By sharing in this way and giving the gift of emotional connectedness, they build a family heritage of grace.

The Good Samaritan

Jesus told the story of the Good Samaritan in response to the question, "Who is my neighbor?" You know the story. Robbers stripped a man, beat him, and left him half-dead on the side of the road. A priest and a Levite, both of whom were men called to serve God, saw the man and crossed the road to avoid him. Perhaps they kept a busy schedule and didn't have time to stop. Perhaps they were fearful that the robbers were still around, waiting to rob anyone who stopped to help. Whatever their reasons, they did not give themselves to the man in need.

A Samaritan saw the injured man on the side of the road and responded differently from the priest or Levite. First, he felt compassion for the injured man. He experienced an emotional connection with the man and, as a result, gave himself to the man. In compassion, the Samaritan made himself available to the man. He did not worry about his busy schedule or the potential dangers of stopping in this part of town. He simply made himself available.

The Samaritan then showed great care and attentiveness to the man's needs. He bandaged his wounds and poured oil and wine on them. He put the man on his own animal and transported him to an inn. The Samaritan stayed with the man the rest of the day and over night to care for his needs. The next day the Samaritan paid the innkeeper to make sure the man was cared for until he recovered fully. The Samaritan was very attentive to this man's needs.

What marks the Samaritan's response as different from the priest's response or the Levite's response? The Samaritan allowed himself to have an emotional connection with the man and then made himself available and attentive to the man's needs. In grace, He gave himself to the wounded man as seen in his availability, attentiveness, and emotional connection.

The Mirror of Grace

When Christ gave Himself for us, He showed Himself available, attentive, and emotionally connected to us. Through the gift of Himself, He ransomed us, redeemed us, and instructed us. When we give ourselves to our family through the investment of our availability, attentiveness, and emotional connectedness, we model what Christ did for us. We will also witness similar results.

Ransoming Power

First, by becoming available and attentive to our family members, we ransom them from a sense of worthlessness. Developmental psychologists suggest that our sense of self develops from the image of ourselves that our loved ones reflect back to us. We become the person we see reflected in the minds of those who love us. If we witness ourselves as valuable in the eyes of those we love, we will grow to see ourselves as lovable. If the actions of those we love reflect a belief in our worth, we come to see ourselves as people of worth.

The act of becoming available and attentive to our family members communicates that we value them. We reflect value and worth to the person to whom we remain available and attentive. In addition, connecting on an emotional level shares a deep love and delight that allows family members to know themselves as loved. So we give ourselves to ransom our family members from a sense of worthlessness and to purchase, with our time and attention, their sense of significance and worth.

With the foundation of availability and the quantity of time spent together, we also increase our influence on family decisions and behavior. Our investment of time allows us to develop a reputation as available and approachable, increasing the likelihood that family members will come to us when they have difficulties or problems for which they seek solutions and support.

When we spend attentive time with family, we learn about each family member's unique abilities, interests, and challenges. We see them in a variety of settings and with a variety of people. They also have the opportunity to observe us in a variety of settings, interacting with a variety of people. As a result, our relationships grow deeper and richer. Relationship skills improve within the family setting and then generalize into the broader community. In this way, our availability and attentiveness ransoms family members from isolation and loneliness, bringing them into intimate relationships and equipping them with the skills they need to enjoy positive social and romantic relationships outside the family.

Families that share emotional connectedness ransom one another from overwhelming emotions run amuck. Specifically, emotional connectedness provides the rich soil in which we learn to manage our emotions. Part of managing emotions is the ability to accept them as a source of information about our priorities and desires but *not* as the single controlling factor in our life. Within an emotionally connected relationship we learn to label and identify the underlying message of our emotions. As we do so, we ransom our family members from the tyranny of emotions. They learn that they do not have to be controlled by overwhelming emotions but are in fact in the driver's seat of those emotions where they can steer the car toward an appropriate Christian response.

By accepting emotions in the safe context of an emotionally connected relationship, we also ransom family members from a sense of inauthenticity. Our emotional connectedness communicates our acceptance of their emotions and conveys the belief that we value them as real people with real emotions.

Redeeming Power

Our availability to family members also liberates them from "lawless deeds." The time we spend with our family members allows us to model the lifestyle that we want them to live. Family members have the opportunity to witness our example in a variety of settings: work and play, church and leisure, winning and losing, good times and bad. The more time we spend with them, the more opportunities they have to witness the lifestyle we consistently attempt to live out and the more opportunities arise in which we can teach the benefits of that lifestyle.

In spite of all of our efforts, family members will at times "miss the mark". We *all* fall short. In these moments, our availability communicates a love that transcends mistakes, shortcomings, and even inappropriate behavior. Even more, remaining emotionally connected through disappointment allows us to discuss what makes various behaviors appropriate or inappropriate and, together, to establish limits to encourage appropriate Christ-like behavior.

Attentive families also redeem one another from lawless deeds. When family members are attentive to one another they no longer feel the need to compete for attention. They find that there is "enough attention to go around." Young girls no longer have to promiscuously seek attention from males outside the family; they know they can receive quality attention from Dad. Young boys do not have to seek attention through delinquent behavior; they know they have a place to belong and are attended to and valued in their family. Spouses do not seek to meet their needs with someone outside the marital relationships because they know their spouse provides the attention and love they so desire.

In addition, family members learn to gain attention through positive behavior. The need for excessive competition disappears, and family members have no need to "act out" or exhibit extreme behaviors to gain attention. Each person in the attentive family knows that he is loved and valued, significant and worthy of attention.

Finally, emotional connectivity teaches family members to recognize emotions in others and respond accordingly. If one family member feels sad, others will recognize and respond appropriately to the emotional expression. Family members will "rejoice with those who rejoice and weep with those who weep" (Romans 12:15). We will also become aware of times when family members are drifting from God and help call them back to godly living and hold them accountable.

Power to Instruct

Grace instructs us to "deny ungodliness and worldly desires and to live sensibly, godly, and righteously" (Titus 2:11-14). When we invest our availability, attentiveness, and emotional connectivity in our family members, we provide a backdrop for doing as the passage above instructs us to do within the family. As we noted earlier, we become the person we see reflected in the minds of those who love us. If we witness ourselves as valuable in the eyes of those we love, we will grow to see ourselves as lovable. If the actions of those we love reflect a belief in our worth, we come to see ourselves as people of value. Remaining available and attentive communicates that we see our family members as valuable and worthy of our time and attention. Against this backdrop, family members experience a greater desire to engage in behaviors that the family deems appropriate. We become better people in response to the gracious love we experience through the availability, attentiveness, and emotional connectedness of our family members.

Greg related an incident in which he was bike riding with one of his friends in high school. He had suggested they ride to a quarry. His friend refused to go because "it would make my parents mad." At the time, Greg was amazed. "Who cares what your parents would think? They won't know." Looking back as an adult, Greg realized that his friend's behavior spoke volumes about his family relationships. His friend did not want to displease his parents who, through their availability, attentiveness, and emotional connectedness, had communicated value, significance, and love to him. His family's gracious gift of themselves had instructed him in "sensible living."

THE PINNACLE OF GRACE

. . . .

"To fully sanctify the marital relationship, we must live it together as Jesus lived his life—embracing the discipline of sacrifice and service as a daily practice. In the same way that Jesus gave His body for us, we are to lay down our energy, our bodies, and our lives for others."

–Gary Thomas

Jesus Christ "gave Himself *to* us" by making Himself available, attentive, and emotionally connected to us. He not only remained available, attentive, and emotionally connected to us, He made sacrifices for us as well. He "gave Himself up for us" (Ephesians 5:25). Paul tells us that Jesus "emptied Himself" (Philippians 2:7) to become a man. He gave up His power—the power of almighty God—to become a human baby cared for by His mother. He gave up His heavenly home for an earthly body. He gave up His life to die on a cross. He sacrificed Himself for us.

Jesus Christ "gave Himself" up to create a heritage of grace for us. If we want to have an intentional Christian family that continues to abide in that heritage of grace, we need to include this sacrificial grace in our family life. We not only need to *give ourselves to* our families but we also need to *give ourselves up* for our families. By doing so, we reach the pinnacle of grace within our family.

Reaching this pinnacle of grace demands that we confront our selfishness. Sacrificial grace does just that. It teaches us to put aside our own personal agenda for the benefit of our families. Sacrifice within the family demonstrates a willingness to set aside self-centered interests to promote the interests of the family, encouraging healthy family relationships. Personal sacrifice for the family acknowledges that you are not in the relationship for what you can *get* but rather for what you can *give*.

Selfless acts of sacrifice also express a deep value for other family members and symbolize our devotion to the family. They increase trust and commitment within the family. Overall, families grow more intimate and secure as family members show a willingness to sacrifice their own desires for the interests of the family.

Giving In

I do, however, want to advise you to exercise some caution when practicing self-sacrifice. All perceived sacrifice is not equal, and some have misused the virtue of sacrifice in harmful ways. For instance, families might teach "giving in" rather than "giving up." Rather than encouraging mutual sacrifice (in which family members give themselves up for one another, which is a gracious gift given in joy), these families demand that one person "give in" to another person's desires. As a result, the person does not sacrifice but rather "gives in" involuntarily to the other person's demands.

"Giving in" results when the person demanding the sacrifice does not put aside his own self-centered agenda but, instead, finds a way to make family members comply with his own demands. The demanding person may make use of the sheer force of his personality or use charm or clever manipulation to make the other person "give in." In more extreme cases, they may induce guilt or threaten physical harm to make others "give in."

Simply "giving in" teaches family members that one's worth comes only from meeting some other person's selfish desires to the neglect of his own personal or developmental needs. Family members who learn to "give in" lose sight of themselves. Their whole identity becomes tied up in meeting the other person's demands. They don't know who they are without those demands to shape their behavior and define their identity. Unfortunately, they may also feel trapped and unable to grow, contributing to a growing disconnection within themselves and a loss of personal identity. Anger and resentment burn as they strive to find a way out of the prison of the other person's demands. As their resentment creates distance in their relationships they grow increasingly isolated and alone. They will likely turn eventually to rebellion to escape.

Sally's family encouraged "giving in." Her father was a well-known and respected leader in the community. He had developed a reputation for strong family values and "couldn't afford" to lose that reputation. Perhaps it was the fear of losing the community's respect that led him to insist that his family "live right." As a child, Sally had to "give in" to certain clothing styles and activities. Initially, Sally "gave in" to her father's expectations because of his strong personality. By the time she reached her pre-teens, however, personality alone was not enough to force compliance. So her father resorted to guilt and shame—saying such things as "If you really loved me you would…" or "I have a reputation to uphold and if you…"—to manipulate her to "give in."

Sally was never encouraged to think about her choices. She was never given the opportunity to voluntarily "give up" things to show her father how much she loved him. As you can imagine, being forced to "give in" only made Sally angry. Eventually, she rebelled against all of his demands in an effort to be her own person instead of merely "the person he wants me to be."

As an adult, Sally stopped rebelling and started working to "get her life back on track." As part of that process, she reflected on her early years of "giving in" and how this influenced her rebellion.

"I love my Dad," she said. "I just had to go wild to get free. Maybe if we could have talked.…If he would have just talked to me and helped me think about things instead of *making* me do it *his way*, I don't know… maybe I would have done a lot of things he asked. I loved him."

As a child, Sally "gave in" to her father's expectations due to the force of his domineering personality. She never had the opportunity to make sacrifices for her family. She never had the opportunity to develop a personal identity aside from the expectations and demands to which she had "given in." Instead, she was forced to "give in" to the identity her father determined for her. As in Sally's life, forcing others to "give in" often leads to a loss of personal identity, a growing resentment, and, eventually, rebellion.

John and Sue hit it off from the moment they met. They quickly drifted into dating and then moved in together. They rationalized that living together was more convenient and less expensive. Secretly, Sue hoped the move would make John happy. She always sensed that she could not live up to John's expectations. Though he never made verbal demands, somehow she knew that she had to change to keep him in her life. So she "gave in" to his unspoken demands. She changed how she dressed and how she styled her hair. She started working out to look the way he wanted her to look. She quit smoking and left her family behind. Still, John never seemed satisfied. No matter how much she "gave in" to his expectations, she never felt he was satisfied with her. Over time, she became angry about his lack of acceptance. Her resentment grew and they began to fight more. One night she had had enough. In the midst of an argument, she packed her bags and left.

Sue had "given in" to satisfy John's unspoken demands and expectations rather than graciously "giving up" in love. Initially, "giving in" seemed the easiest way to get what she wanted—John's love and acceptance. The gracious act of true sacrifice would have demanded that she somehow confront the real issue—his level of acceptance—and potentially lose what she desired most. In "giving in" she lost herself in bitterness and resentment. As that bitterness took root, her relationship with John grew more distant until she lost what she most desired—intimacy with John.

When we "give in," for whatever reason, we lose ourselves in the process. Resentment and anger take root and create a growing distance in relationships that often ends in rebellion. True sacrificial giving has the opposite result. People who willingly "give up" for others develop a stronger and more mature personal identity. In addition, true sacrifice promotes the trust that builds strong relationships and leads to a more secure knowledge of ourselves.

Playing the Martyr

Other families mistake martyrdom for sacrifice. Rather than willingly "give up" for the other person with pure motives, they play the martyr. Those who play the martyr "give up" begrudgingly, with an ulterior motive of being recognized for their great gift of sacrifice. They make sure everyone notices their sacrifice as they complain about the price they pay and how thankless it is because their great sacrifices go unnoticed. They become judgmental of everyone else and assume everyone else judges them. Perhaps they do this to cover up their own insecurities and fears.

As time goes on, martyrs become exhausted and burned out. In their exhaustion, they feel taken advantage of and unappreciated, victimized by those for whom they have "sacrificed." Martyrs then lose themselves and their sense of identity as they become overwhelmed with feelings of exhaustion and victimization.

Those around the martyr always feel as though they cannot live up to the martyr's expectations. They never feel "good enough." As a result, they begin to distance themselves from the martyr. Relationships fall by the wayside and intimacy is destroyed.

You can recognize martyrs from the statements they make, which distinguish them from truly gracious sacrificers. Such statements might include:

- "Nobody really cares or appreciates how much I sacrifice for this family."

- "I'll do it. I do everything else around here."

- "I don't want to be a bad Dad, so I'll skip work for you."

- "You ought to be ashamed of yourself after all I've done for you."

- You act like you don't love me. That's fine. Maybe I'll just leave."

Jack used to play the martyr. At times he felt left out and unappreciated, so he made comments such as those above in an effort to "get others to notice." When he looks back, he knows he was not left out or unappreciated. People did care for him and appreciated what he did. He had a loving family and strong friendships. Still, at times he inaccurately perceived himself as "not good enough" and, therefore, felt unappreciated.

Jack always made "sacrifices" for his family, but with the mindset of a martyr. For example, he begrudgingly let his daughter have the best bedroom in the house when they moved, hoping that she would recognize his sacrifice. When she said nothing to pay tribute to his great sacrifice, he complained about being unappreciated. He made comments such as, "We'll do what you want. It doesn't matter what I like anyway…as long as *you* are happy."

As we talked about this mentality, Jack began to understand that playing the martyr and begrudgingly making a "sacrifice" only made him more melancholy and sad. His complaints about his "sacrifice" only drove a wedge between himself and his family, which was the exact opposite of his intent. He didn't want a wedge; he wanted intimacy. That is perhaps the saddest consequence of playing the martyr—the martyr's actions lead to increased melancholy and less intimacy when what the martyr desires most are connection and joy.

Jane also played the martyr in her family. This became more evident after the family went through a series of traumatic circumstances that included job changes, marital separation, and a move. The children began to "act up" in response to the stress. Jane loved her children and tried to make things better. To protect her children from the pain she gave up her own needs to give the children "something extra"—the best clothes, the best room, the best toys. The children, however, continued to misbehave in anger and fear.

Jane became frustrated and began playing the martyr: "No matter what I do, they don't care!" She continued to sacrifice her own needs to give them "something extra." With each gift, she announced two things. First, she made known "what a heavy price" she had paid, how much "she had suffered," and how "hard this situation was for her." Second, she expressed great disappointment that "no one appreciated" all that she did and that "everyone took advantage of her pain and kindness." She emphasized that she "would never treat someone like that, especially if they had done so much for me."

Each time Jane made one of these comments her children either shut down or began arguing. Each time she played the martyr, she drove a wedge between her and her children. She became more resentful and angry. She began to question her feelings and thoughts. She felt less like her real self and more like a person she neither knew nor liked.

That is the result of playing the martyr—distance in relationships, growing anger and resentment, sense of confusion, and loss of identity.

The Rescuer

Some families encourage rescuing rather than true sacrifice. Rescuers have a sincere love for other people. They want the other person to find success and happiness. They also hate to see other people in pain or suffering. Many have a desire for affirmation, stability, and order.

When rescuers see someone in pain, they feel compelled to help. Like the proverbial white knight, they ride in to save the day. Since they cannot bear to see the other person suffer, they may cover up that person's negative behavior. After all, the rescuer has remedied the situation and made it all better, saved the person from the immediate consequences, and everything is back in order…stability restored.

Unfortunately, the rescued person learns nothing. He returns to his inappropriate behavior confident that that rescuer will be there to clean up whatever mess he makes. When it happens, the rescuer steps in to save the day again. Over and over, the rescuer swoops in to act as personal savior. He gives his time and energy to rescue the person in need, but all the efforts bring only temporary stability and order to the people involved.

In essence, rescuers *appear* to make "sacrifices." But alas they have ulterior motives. The desire to save the other person, and maybe even to change him, is what motivates the rescuer to take action. Rescuers are also motivated by the desire to gain stability and order in their lives and the lives of those they rescue. Motivation stems from a secret desire that the changed person and stable situation will gain the rescuer the affirmation he desires.

Sadly, their efforts do not work. Rescuers are enablers. Rather than changing the other person, they simply enable him to continue in the negative behavior. The rescuer then feels like a failure, powerless to bring about the desired change or stability. Continued "sacrifice" with the goal of saving the other person leads to exhaustion. The rescuer's own needs go unmet and his anger grows. Not surprisingly, relationships suffer and intimacy is destroyed.

Rescuers teach family members hypocrisy. Family members learn to portray a false self in which they behave one way in public while covering up what they do not want others to know. They often present a confident, self-assured image when inside they feel like a worthless failure. This split image interferes with the development of a solid identity. The rescuer's identity becomes wrapped up in the other person's behavior and, if the other person changes, the rescuer is left with no identity.

Hanna loved her brother. She would do anything to rescue him from the consequences of his poor decisions and bring stability into his life and, by proxy, into her family's life. She quit going out with friends so she could supervise him and help him avoid getting in bad situations. She gave him money to pay *his* bills after he spent all his money on gambling and video games. She spent days cleaning his apartment before his landlord evicted him for the filth. The more she rescued her brother, the more dependent her brother seemed to become. When she tried to quit doing so much for him, he would start to falter and she would feel guilty.

Other people initially thought she seemed fine. Beneath her happy façade, however, she felt like a failure. Nothing she did brought the change and stability she sought. This also contributed to her feeling insecure, wondering if she was really good at anything. She grew more fearful as her brother did less and less. She began to wonder if she could really keep this up. At times, she felt as though it would kill her if she had to continue this way. Her relationships with other people began to fade as she focused all her attention on "fixing" her brother's broken life. Anger began to grow and resentment took root. "How could he do this to me? I have sacrificed so much and he doesn't even appreciate it. He's just using me!" As her anger and insecurity grew, so did his. Their relationship became strained. They were caught in a bitter cycle of her trying to rescue him and his becoming more dependent on her help to survive.

Rescuers truly care for other people. They are willing to give up almost anything to help a person in need. Their sacrifice, however, is lost in their effort to *make* the other person change. They act as though they are "responsible for" the other person's decision-making and success or failure rather than "responsible to" be kind, considerate, and fair towards the other person. They strive to maintain stability and order while protecting others from the chaos of their own actions. In the short-term, everything looks good. In the long-run, the rescuer becomes increasingly "responsible for" a dependent other and contributes to increasing the dependency, which hurts everyone. They become exhausted trying to provide for everyone else's needs while ignoring their own. Rescuers lose their identity and their self-image plummets as their heroic efforts bring no lasting results. Eventually, intimacy is destroyed and the rescuer feels like a frustrated failure.

True Sacrifice

Members of the intentional Christian family do not "give in," play the martyr, or rescue. Instead, they willingly sacrifice for one another just as Christ "gave Himself up" for us. First, family members become available, attentive, and emotionally connected to give themselves to their family. Then to further express grace they freely put aside their own agenda in order to strengthen the family through sacrifice. They sacrifice willingly, setting aside their personal interests to promote the family's interests. Unlike the rescuer, the true sacrificer has no ulterior motive. They do not expect the other to change in response to their sacrifices. Nor do they seek affirmation because they make their sacrifices freely with no strings attached and with no expectation of return.

Unlike the martyr the true sacrificer does not complain; there is no "woe is me."True sacrificers do not begrudge making a sacrifice. In fact, they experience joy in sacrificing for their family. Their sacrifice expresses the deep value they place on the family and family members. It also symbolizes devotion to the family, increases personal security within the family, and strengthens overall family stability.

Rather than losing their identity, those who make true sacrifices for their family members grow more mature and secure in their identity. Rather than insecurity, those who make true sacrifices experience greater commitment and security within the family. They experience acceptance and trust in the family, which results in greater intimacy and devotion.

True sacrifice teaches family members the joy of giving oneself to others. It teaches that our personal worth rests in the fact that we are a magnificent creation of God and thus worthy of love. True sacrifice brings joy, satisfaction, and renewed energy. It builds on the heritage of grace that Christ modeled during His life on earth.

Mike and his wife both worked long hours in high-pressure jobs. Mike was promoted to a supervisory position at the local community mental health clinic where he worked. He was an excellent employee and an outstanding manager who motivated his staff to excellence. One day Mike came out of a meeting with our boss and announced that he had resigned. As we discussed his resignation, he talked about his children and his family. He shared how his children had begun to ask why neither parent could come to their school functions or practice sessions. They wanted a parent present. Mike and his wife discussed their children's concern and determined that the family could afford for him to resign. Mike loved his family so much that he sacrificed his career and paycheck to provide a stable and supportive home environment for their children. He put his career ambitions on hold for a period of time in order to strengthen his family.

I saw Mike about a year later and asked him about his decision. He said it was the best decision he had ever made. His face radiated with joy and pride as he spoke about his children and their lives. His smile spanned from ear to ear as he discussed his wife's career and his support of that career. Mike was truly happy. He had grown stronger in his personal identity and he was enjoying the fruits of a stable, happy home that shared a heritage of grace.

Giving In	Playing the Martyr	Rescuers	True Sacrifice
Unwillingly "gives in" to other person's demands	Gives time and energy begrudgingly	Gives time and energy with the goal of changing the other person, gaining personal stability/order, or gaining affirmation	Willingly sets aside personal interests to promote the family's interests
Person forced to "give in" in response to: other person's strong personality, guilt, physical threats	Complains while making apparent sacrifice	Person feels powerless, insecure, and a failure as efforts do not bring desired results	Expresses deep value for family and family members, increases stability and security within family

Teaches that personal worth is found only when meeting others' needs and demands	Teaches you can never measure up, you are never "good enough," always falling short	Teaches to portray a false self, to look confident and self-assured while feeling worthless, to be "responsible for" rather than "responsible to" others	Teaches family members to value others and teaches them the joy of giving of self to others
Loss of identity, self-image plummets as insecurity increases	Loss of identity, self-image plummets, person becomes self-absorbed and judgmental to hide insecurities	Loss of identity, self-image plummets as feel like efforts make no impact	Grows more secure in personal identity and more mature in general
Feel increased anger and resentment, eventually rebel	Feel taken advantage of, exhausted, unappreciated, and victimized	Feel exhausted, needs go unmet, may eventually strike out in anger	Feel increased joy and satisfaction
Intimacy destroyed, relationship lost	Burned out, more melancholy, and intimacy destroyed	Intimacy destroyed	Increased trust, commitment, devotion, and intimacy

12 FORGIVENESS

....

"Sin in marriage (on the part of both spouses) is a daily reality, an ongoing struggle that threatens to hold us back. You will never find a spouse who is without sin. The person you decide to marry will eventually hurt you—sometimes even intentionally so, making forgiveness an essential spiritual discipline."

—Gary Thomas

"Be kind to one another, tender-hearted, forgiving each other just as God in Christ also has forgiven you."

–Ephesians 4:32

Building a family heritage of grace begins with acceptance. Unconditional acceptance sets the stage for grace. Grace begins when we make ourselves available, attentive, and emotionally connected to our family members. Sacrifice—the giving ourselves up for our family—moves us to the pinnacle of grace. All of this combines to build a strong family heritage of grace.

It all sounds straightforward, but there is a catch. Families are made up of people, sinful people. Sooner or later, family members hurt one another, *sometimes even intentionally.* As a result, forgiveness becomes an integral and crucial aspect of maintaining the family heritage of grace.

Without forgiveness, broken relationships remain broken and may even grow more difficult to repair. The unforgiving victim actually holds the offender in bondage, creating a one-up relationship potentially filled with acts of vengeance. For instance, the victim may try to "make the offender pay" for what he did or "never let him live it down." The unforgiving victim will always feel as though the offender owes him something. As he ruminates about the injustice done to him, he may demand a just recompense. He may exact justice by making demands of the offender (with punitive intent) or by avoiding the offender altogether. Unfortunately, none of these actions will satisfy the victim. No amount of repayment can ever truly erase the offense. After all, what action or payment could truly compensate for hurt emotions or a momentary loss of trust? As a result, the unforgiving victim finds that he and the offender are bound together, cellmates locked up in a common prison of bitterness, anger, and hate.

Lack of forgiveness also affects relationships outside the victim-offender relationship. As the victim dwells on how he was hurt, he begins to see signs of it everywhere. He indiscriminately casts stones of revenge at strangers, friends, and family members each time an innocent facial expression, tone of voice, circumstance, or wrong word suddenly arouses the anger he harbors against the original offender. In other words, anger and bitter resentment consume the victim. It grows like a cancer and will choke the life out of the person who refuses to let it go in forgiveness. Even more, it grows to infest every other relationship and interaction the unforgiving person has, leaving him bitter, angry, and ultimately alone. Perhaps that is why Paul said to "let all bitterness and wrath and anger and clamor and slander be put away from you…" just before telling his readers to "be kind hearted to one another, tender-hearted, forgiving each other, just as God in Christ also has forgiven you" (Ephesians 4:31-32).

The writer of Hebrews went so far as to tell his readers, "See to it that no one comes short of the grace of God; that no root of bitterness springing up causes trouble, and by it many be defiled" (Hebrews 12:15). Notice that bitterness is associated with falling short of God's grace. Bitterness causes trouble, not just for the one who harbors the bitterness but for the "many" around him. A lack of forgiveness allows bitterness to take root and through it the whole family suffers. Forgiveness, on the other hand, relieves us of bitterness and brings a healing balm to the family, strengthening a heritage of grace.

The Call to Forgive

Jesus taught His followers about forgiveness several times during His earthly ministry. When teaching His disciples to pray, He told them to pray "forgive us our sins as we forgive everyone who is indebted to us" (Luke 11:4). In the Sermon on the Mount, Jesus followed this teaching on the prayer of forgiveness with these familiar words: "…if you forgive men for their transgressions, your heavenly Father will also forgive you. But if you do not forgive men, then your Father will not forgive your transgressions" (Matthew 6:14-15). Mark's gospel also records Jesus' teaching that effective prayer demands that we forgive those who have sinned against us (Mark 11:25-26). Jesus commands us to forgive. A lack of forgiveness hinders our prayers to God and prevents us from receiving God's forgiveness ourselves.

Jesus' teaching on forgiveness went even further. When Peter asked Him how often a person should forgive, Jesus basically told him to forgive as many times as someone sinned against him. He then told the parable of an unforgiving servant (Matthew 18:21-35) in which a king forgave his servant the debt of a huge sum of money, more than he could ever repay. This servant thanked the king but then went out and demanded that a second servant repay him a much smaller debt. Some commentators believe that these two debts may have been as different as 1,000,000 to 1; the unforgiving servant may have owed $1,000,000 to the king for every $1 the second servant owed him. Amazingly, the first servant demanded payment even after receiving such extravagant forgiveness. The king heard about this and threw the unforgiving servant in jail to be tortured for his lack of forgiveness. Jesus ended the parable by saying, "So shall my heavenly Father also do to you, if each of you does not forgive his brother from your heart" (Matthew 18:35).

God has forgiven us a huge debt, more than we could ever repay. In turn, He expects us to forgive those who sin against us. God has forgiven us 1,000,000 sins for every 1 sin we might have to forgive another person. If we remain unforgiving, we risk losing our eternal home with God. Bitterness and anger will torture us and separate us from others and, eventually, from God.

Realizing the extravagance of God's forgiveness can help us forgive others. Jesus helped Simon, a Pharisee, understand this lesson. Simon had invited Jesus to his home for dinner. While eating, a sinful woman came in, anointed Jesus' feet with her tears and perfume, and then wiped His feet clean with her hair before massaging His feet with her kisses. Simon was appalled that Jesus would let this sinful woman touch Him. Jesus told a story to address Simon's concern. In the story a man offered two debtors forgiveness. One debtor was forgiven a debt of about two years' wages and the other was forgiven a debt of about two months' wages. Jesus then asked Simon which debtor would love the man more? Simon told Jesus that the debtor who was forgiven the greater debt would of course feel greater love. Jesus then said, "Her sins, which are many, are forgiven, for she loved much; but he who is forgiven little, loves little" (Luke 7:47).

We know the joy of extravagant forgiveness that God offers in response to our countless sinful acts. To make such extreme forgiveness possible

Jesus paid the extreme price of His blood and life. In response, we love dearly and we forgive freely, just as He so dearly loved and so freely forgave us. How can we do any less? That is the command of God in Christ and, as such, is crucial to building a heritage of grace within our families.

Benefits of Forgiveness

In His infinite wisdom God gives us various commandments for our benefit. He knows that forgiveness will help us live life abundantly. Researchers in our day are discovering that very truth. Their findings confirm that holding on to bitterness results in long-term health problems whereas forgiveness offers many benefits. For instance, forgiveness can lower blood pressure, reduce stress, decrease hostility, and lower heart rate. What's more, those who forgive are at lower risk for drug and alcohol abuse, depressive symptoms, and anxiety symptoms. They experience less chronic pain and improved psychological well-being. What's more they have more friends and healthier relationships (Mayo Clinic, 2007).

Forgiveness within the family helps to create an environment of greater emotional stability and higher conscientiousness. It also promotes agreeableness between family members and more conversation (Maio et al., 2008). In other words, forgiveness seems to create a spiraling effect of growing intimacy and concern for other family members. Forgiveness contributes to a greater willingness to make sacrifices for the sake of family relationships as well as a greater willingness to make personal changes that will have a positive impact on one's relational and physical health. So what exactly is forgiveness?

What Exactly is Forgiveness?

Forgiveness involves a decision to let go of a record of wrongs as well as the demand for revenge and actively replace negative feelings such as bitterness and resentment with more positive feelings such as compassion, benevolence, and love. Forgiveness produces not only a change in emotions toward the offender but a change in behavior as well. Let's explore this definition in more detail. To help others better understand forgiveness, I often use two props: a brick and a rope. If possible, find a brick and a rope to use as we go through the example now.

Imagine that you have a disagreement with your friend. In anger, your friend tells a lie about you, a rumor that defames your reputation. Believing the rumor, people begin to treat you differently. Your friend has lied about you. He has sinned against you. You are hurt and angry. Rather than offer forgiveness, you want justice! After all, he is guilty of sin. He has ruined your reputation. You want to see him punished. Justice demands punishment. He must pay the price for his sin. Figuratively, the demand for just punishment is like picking up a rock with which to stone him. When I work with people on forgiveness, I actually hand them a brick (or an iron, a heavy candle, or some other heavy object) to hold at this point. So, pick up your brick. Hold it in one hand to represent your righteous stone of judgment.

As you hold your stone of judgment in one hand, contemplate how much he has wronged you and how much he owes you. He is indebted to you because of his sin and will remain indebted to you until he pays his debt. Unfortunately, the debt you hold ties you to him like a rope. Once again, as I explain this concept to people, I tie one end of a rope to the person's wrist and the other to a chair that represents the offender. Go ahead, tie one end of your rope to your wrist and the other to a chair to represent the rope of bitter debt tying you to the past.

Now you find yourself weighed down by the stone of judgment and anger in one hand and tied to the past with the rope of bitter debt on the other hand. When you attempt to move into the future, the rope of unforgiven debt holds you back and tightens around your wrist like a choke collar on a dog. When you attempt to show someone soft, loving emotions, the stones of judgment weigh you down and the rope of unforgiven debt holds you back.

You can only escape this trap by practicing forgiveness. You must make a conscious choice to let go of the stones of judgment, releasing the need for revenge and punishment. Then, in an altruistic act of grace, untie the rope of bitter debt and replace any negative emotions you have toward the other person with the positive emotions of acceptance and grace. Free of the burden of the stones of judgment and the restrictions of the rope of bitter debt, you can freely move into the future.

But How?

Everett Worthington developed a five-step model to help people "REACH" forgiveness (2001). In general, this model promotes forgiveness by teaching the victim to recall (R) the offense in an objective manner, build empathy (E) for the offender, altruistically (A) offer forgiveness, commit (C) to forgiveness and then hold (H) on to that forgiveness. Perhaps a closer look at these five components will help us incorporate the grace of forgiveness into our families.

Recall the hurt

The initial step in the process of forgiveness may at first glance appear counterintuitive. You need to recall the offense against you, however, and objectively define what you have lost because of the sin. Do not allow yourself to think of the offender as evil and do not ruminate on how you *feel* about this wrong. Instead, objectively define how the offense has impacted you. In completing this objective recounting of the wrong committed against you, you may well realize that you truly do have a right to expect justice.

Empathize with the offender

In the second step of forgiveness, you must empathize with the offender. Take time to understand him or her and to consider his or her human condition. Like us, the one who sinned against you is one of God's fallen creations, held in the abusive grip of Satan until Christ sets him free. Consider the pain and the blindness that may have led him or her to sin against you.

Some theorists suggest that a person can promote empathy by exploring several aspects about the offender (Bolt, 2004). First, list 3 or 4 things about the offender's past that may have contributed to his propensity to sin in that particular manner. Second, imagine what the offender may have been thinking or feeling when the offense occurred. Third, consider how the offender's life may be worse now as a result of the offense. How has this sin impacted his life? Finally, allow yourself to recall your relationship with the offender beyond the offense. Describe 2 or 3 positive memories you may have of the offender, 2 or 3 positive traits you may have seen in the offender, and 2 or 3 times the offender has shown good judgment.

Reviewing your answers to these questions may help you turn bitterness into compassion and the desire for revenge into a desire for his deliverance. You can entrust your desire for justice to a "righteous judge" (1 Peter 2:23) and offer forgiveness instead (Luke 24:34). In grace, you can bear his weakness to God in prayer.

Altruistic Forgiveness

Next, offer the altruistic gift of forgiveness. This is an altruistic action, a gift of grace. To help you complete this step, recall a time when you sinned against another person, felt genuine guilt for your actions, and received forgiveness from that person. Remember how grateful you felt for this undeserved gift.

Take this a step further and recall how often you have sinned against God. Each day we sin multiple times against our Creator. Any sin committed against us pales in comparison to our sin against God. Yet, God, in His mercy and grace, offers us forgiveness. With this understanding, it becomes morally hypocritical to refuse the altruistic gift of forgiveness to the family member who hurt us.

We follow Christ's example when we humbly lay down our right to exact revenge and drop the stones of angry judgment. In humility, we make a conscious decision to lay down our own stone of judgment and leave the final judgment to a perfect God who is a Righteous Judge (1 Peter 2:21-24), trusting Him to balance justice and mercy. Isn't that what Jesus did when He came to earth? Although God demands justice, in Jesus He also accepted the just consequence of our sin. He demanded a just payment for sin and, at the same time, made that payment for us. Jesus Christ paid the debt of sin we had accrued. In so doing, He became the Just and the Justifier of our forgiveness. We follow His example when we offer the altruistic gift of forgiveness to our family members.

Commit to forgiving

After you have offered the altruistic gift of forgiveness, you need to commit to that forgiveness. This may involve making your commitment to forgive public. Tell the offender, tell a friend, write it down, whatever it takes to let others know you are committed to living out forgiveness in relation to the other person.

In this step, we follow God's example of committing Himself to forgive us. He designed and initiated the plan to make forgiveness possible and sent Jesus to earth to complete the plan. God, the very one whom we had sinned against, initiated forgiveness, not the one who needed forgiveness. The one who owed the debt did not pay the debt. Instead, the one to whom the debt was owed paid the debt Himself! The one needing forgiveness did not approach God and ask for it; God initiated the forgiveness and forgave first.

I often hear people say something to this effect: "I'll forgive her when she apologizes." God did not wait for us to realize our sin and apologize. He initiated and carried out the actions of forgiveness *before* we sought that forgiveness. He died on the cross to pay the debt for our sins while we were still sinners. We must accept that work to restore our relationship with Him, yes, but He already paid the price.

To forgive others in the same manner as God forgives us, we must initiate the act of forgiveness rather than wait for the other person to apologize or show remorse. We simply offer forgiveness as our heavenly Father offered forgiveness to us. We cut the rope of bitter debt that ties us to the offender and offer forgiveness. These actions commit us to living out our forgiveness.

Hold on to Forgiveness

Jeremiah quotes God as saying, "I will forgive their iniquity, and their sin I will remember no more" (Jeremiah 31:34). I like that Jeremiah says that God will "remember our sin no more" instead of He will "forget it." God does not passively forget. He makes the intentional decision and effort to remember it no more. He replaces the thought of our sin with the thought of our place in His plan. He replaces the thought of our sin with the thought of our redemption through Christ. He remembers our sin no more but instead remembers our trust in, and love for, Christ!

When we offer forgiveness, our minds will bring up the offense time and again. Satan will attempt to convince us that we should pick up the dropped stones of angry judgment and retie the rope of bitter debt. When that occurs, we need to choose to "remember their sin no more." We can take those thoughts captive for Jesus Christ (2 Corinthians 10:5) and replace them with God's forgiveness for us and our forgiveness for him or her.

Conclusion

Our families are made up of sinful people just like you and me. Fortunately, this gives us the opportunity to practice grace by forgiving one another as Christ forgave us. In some case we can forgive easily. A minor offense presents little difficulty. In other cases, however, the offense is significant and forgiveness becomes more difficult. Either way, building a family heritage of grace demands that we forgive "even as Christ also has forgiven you."

13 GRACE AND DISCIPLINE

"For the grace of God has appeared, bringing salvation to all men, instructing us to deny ungodliness and worldly desires and to live sensibly, righteously and godly in the present age...."

–Titus 2:11-14

It always happens at the worst time. I just wanted to take a short stroll through town, stretch my legs, and share time with my family before finishing the long drive. As my family and I walked down the street, however, a man and woman approached us. They claimed to be traveling to the man's hometown to visit his dying mother. Unfortunately, they had left home in a hurry and, because they were so distraught about his mother's illness, had forgotten to bring extra money. Their car was out of gas and they were stranded. All they wanted was to get home to see the man's poor mother before she died. "Could you please spare some change so we could buy a tank of gas to get home to her?"

You know, I love to help people. I want to help people. I believe it is an act of grace to reach out to those in need and offer assistance. I would love to have enough resources to simply give everyone assistance with no need of repayment. The easiest thing would have been to reach into my pocket, offer a quick donation, and continue on my way feeling good about my gracious generosity. But that misses the point of true grace. That is a lazy grace, a misunderstanding of true, instructive grace. I have to tell you, I find it much easier to practice lazy grace.

I also find it easier to listen to the benefits of grace. I love to hear a testimony in which people tell the story of their redemption, salvation, and eternal relationship with a loving, gracious God. Such testimonies often begin with the description of a lost sinner, drowning in some dramatic sin such as drunkenness, sexual promiscuity, or some other life-compromising circumstance. Suddenly, the grace of God appears bringing salvation, redemption from sin, and abundant life in Christ.

When I was young I used to wish my testimony was more like that, a more exciting rendition of God's grace. Instead, my testimony consists of growing up in a Christian home, meeting Christ at a young age, remaining involved with Him throughout my life, and loving Him even when I missed the mark and sinned. I have since come to realize that a testimony such as mine really is a testimony of great grace. At the time, however, those dramatic testimonies taught me that grace increases where sin increases (Romans 5:20) and... I would have liked to receive more grace. I had the mistaken idea that Paul addresses when he asked, "Are we to continue in sin that grace might increase?" and then answered by saying, "May it never be!" (Romans 6:1-2).

Grace does not mean that we allow sin and misbehavior. A family heritage of grace does not simply look the other way when people sin or misbehave. A grace-filled family does not allow an immature child to lie or engage in a tantrum without consequences. No, the grace-filled family seizes those moments as opportunities to instruct in "sensible, righteous, and godly" living. True grace demands discipline.

Gracious families know that we all sin. They accept the sinner and courageously enter into the struggle to overcome sin. Family members turn toward one another and work to bring sin into the light of Christ in order to produce more mature, Christ-like behavior. In other words, gracious families train one another in self-control (denying ungodliness and worldly desires) and character (to live sensibly, righteously, and godly).

Previous chapters in this section on grace described the way in which grace benefits the family and how the family can build a positive heritage of grace. Those chapters focused on the positive aspects of grace that I love—acceptance, giving ourselves, and sacrifice. But I have to tell you that I find it much more difficult to talk about the hard aspects of grace—the instructive side of grace. Grace does indeed instruct us, however, and disciplines us to live sensibly, godly, and righteously.

The last chapter addressed forgiveness, specifically, how to respond with grace after someone has sinned against us. This chapter focuses on discipline—how to instruct one another in an effort to prevent sin in the future. As we discuss discipline, remember that grace involves acceptance. A truly gracious family offers unconditional acceptance. We always accept one another as God's wonderful creations, His masterpiece, created in His image. We always extend this acceptance to the person. Acceptance does not extend to the sinful behavior, however. Although a gracious family accepts one another, shortcomings and all, it also strives to overcome those shortcomings and train each person to become more Christ-like in word and deed.

Grace also demands that we remain available, attentive, and emotionally connected to one another. Having this attitude will affect how we "instruct" one another in "sensible, godly, and righteous" behavior. We have to keep these basic aspects of grace in mind as we explore how grace fits together with discipline in building our family heritage of grace. Unfortunately, not all families maintain these aspects of grace in the midst of discipline. Remember the grace rejecters, grace crushers, and grace manipulators? They don't practice grace in discipline. Only the grace receivers learn to discipline with grace.

Grace Rejecters

Grace rejecters trust in their own ability. They strive to define themselves through achievements and possessions, both of which become symbols of success. As a result, they are very busy people. Grace rejecters often become image-conscious. They do not want to be seen as lazy, unsuccessful, or inadequate. They become so caught up in the busyness that creates and maintains their image and defines their person that they do not have time either to give or to accept grace. They miss grace because their eyes focus selfishly on the priority of a successful image.

Grace rejecters do not have time for problem behavior and therefore deal with it several ways. First, grace rejecters may ignore the person who engages in the problem behavior and withdraw love from him or her. After giving a consequence for the behavior, grace rejecters abandon the misbehaving person rather than empathize with him. In this way, the grace rejecter takes away both the offending person's hope of love and acceptance and his opportunity to grow.

Second, in the eyes of the grace-rejecting family, misbehavior threatens the family's image and identity. Grace rejecters often assume that the misbehaving person intentionally misbehaved to make them look bad. They become embarrassed and angry and in their anger, they attack the misbehaving member's character rather than addressing the misbehavior. They may also nag the misbehaving person to act in accordance with the "real family image" and make guilt-inducing comments when they do not live up to that standard.

Luke lived in a grace-rejecting family. One day he used foul language. His father responded with an attack on Luke's character. He called him demeaning names and stated that his behavior revealed a desire to make the family look bad. He imposed a severe punishment (not discipline). I cannot quote him directly because of the inappropriate words he used, but the gist of it was something like: "Luke, you are a lazy loser and you keep proving it to me. You never listen. And you make the whole family look bad. You are pathetic. You are grounded from the Internet, TV, phone, and friends, indefinitely." His father then left the room and did not speak to Luke for over a week.

Luke was left with virtually nothing for an undefined period of time. He thought it would be a week or so, but his father had not even spoken to him after a week. He sought out his father to ask him how he could reconcile. He wanted to know how long he had to endure the punishment before regaining some privileges. His father simply replied, "When I say it's over." Luke had no hope of reconciliation or restoration. He was condemned as an eternal lazy loser (among other things) with no opportunity to prove himself otherwise and no hope of reconciliation.

You can imagine Luke's response. He grew depressed. He gave up and decided that if he was in that much trouble he may as well just do whatever he wanted. He no longer cared. His behavior in school got worse and his grades began to drop. He became more disrespectful of his father, avoiding him when he could and talking back to him when he couldn't. This got his father's attention but only increased his punishment.

So the cycle turns in the grace-rejecting family. Instead of providing training in self-control and sound character, the family ignores, demeans, and attacks. They take away the hope of reconciliation and restoration. The "blackballed" person may give up and begin to misbehave because he has no other option for gaining attention or restoring the relationship.

Grace Crushers

Grace crushers do not discipline with grace, either. Grace crushers focus on the rules to the neglect of relationships. They judge one another based on whether a member's performance and behavior meets the legalistic standard established. This leads to either arrogance or shame, depending on whether one meets the standard. Grace-crushing families do not take the time to see each member's unique and special aspects. The members cannot accept the strengths in other family members for fear that doing so will diminish their own uniqueness. Grace crushers do not take each family member's concerns seriously. Each member focuses only on his own concerns and rejects the other members' opinions.

Grace crushers use shame-based discipline. They attempt to "train" one another in self-control and positive character by inducing shame. Such families make statements such as:

- "You ought to be ashamed of yourself."
- "What will the neighbors think?"
- "I'm glad your grandmother isn't here to see this "
- "If you loved me you would never do that."
- "Would Jesus do that? ...I don't think so! "
- "And you call yourself a Christian?"
- "You are such a disappointment."
- "How would you feel if I treated you like that?"
- "You haven't done anything all day except lie around and watch me do all the work."
- "I work all day for you and you treat me like I don't even exist."

Grace crushers use guilt and shame as motivators to produce change. The trouble is, such statements do not work. They simply instill a deep-seated sense of shame that can lead to resentment, a sense of inadequacy, and a constant need for approval from others.

Grace crushers may also use a fear-based style of discipline. Fear-based discipline attempts to "teach" self-control and positive character by inducing fear. Grace crushers may threaten to take away love and attention or they threaten catastrophic consequences in response to misbehavior. Fear-based statements I have heard from such grace-crushing families include:

- "If you keep behaving like this I'll call the police and have them take you away."
- "Why don't we just get a divorce?"
- "I'm going to break that TV if you don't turn it off."
- "I'll just sell that computer if you can't quit."

Like shame-based discipline, fear-based discipline does not produce self-control and positive character. It produces resentment, fear of failure, and fear of trying new things. It also leads to rebellion.

Josh McDowell (2000) coined the formula "rules without relationship equals rebellion." Focusing on rules and attempting to gain compliance with rules through shame and fear produces a sense of inadequacy and a fear that can immobilize a person. Without a foundational loving relationship, rules lead only to resentment, rebellion, and separation.

Grace Manipulators

Grace manipulators discipline with a lazy grace. They focus more on relationship than structure in the naïve belief that simply accepting one another will lead to self-control and strong character. Strong relationships, they believe, erase the need for instructive discipline. Grace manipulators hate to see anyone suffer pain. Practicing a lazy grace, they attempt to protect the misbehaving person from the painful consequences of her inappropriate actions. Grace manipulators also fear that the other person will become angry and frustrated with the consequence and blame them, straining (or perhaps even ending) the relationship. In a sense, the misbehaving person's anger and frustration proves more powerful than her love. It overwhelms the grace manipulator's love, so the grace manipulator responds with a lazy grace.

In order to avoid watching the person suffer discomfort or pain as a result of his behavior, grace manipulators may simply allow inappropriate behavior without imposing any consequences. I ran into this situation while leading a children's church program. One of the young students misbehaved during worship. His behavior was so disruptive that I decided to talk with his mother about his behavior. I told him I would talk to his mother as soon as I cleaned up. I should not have waited. When I approached his mother she spoke first and told me that her son had already told her what had happened. She continued, "Isn't he a good boy? I am so proud of him for telling me how he misbehaved. How can I say anything about his bad behavior since he told me the truth? I don't want him to think I'm punishing him for telling me the truth." She feared that disciplining his behavior would jeopardize her relationship with him or risk his "not telling the truth in the future." As a result, his negative behavior had no consequence. He never experienced the discomfort of his inappropriate and disruptive behavior.

Similarly, grace manipulators may bail family members out rather than allow them to experience the discomfort of negative consequences—even natural and logical consequences of their misbehavior. Grace-manipulating families may accommodate or bank-roll negative behavior to interfere with the consequences. Families that allow angry family members to "blow their stack," call names, or even hit one another without consequence are accommodating negative behavior. So are families that finish a child's project for him because the child refused to do it.

Families that continue to give money to the member who has consistently misused it in the past are bank-rolling negative behavior. So are families that hide the consequences of drunken behavior while continuing to provide alcohol. In both cases, the grace manipulating family is bailing out the misbehaving person to protect him from the consequences of his behavior.

When grace manipulators protect misbehaving family members from the consequences of their behavior, they end up suffering the consequences themselves. For example, the parent who stays up late to finish a child's project while the child sleeps will suffer the pain of frustration and fatigue. The child simply reaps the benefit of a finished project without ever learning to plan better or work harder. The grace manipulator has taken the problem as his own rather than allowing the misbehaving person to own his own misbehavior.

Protecting the misbehaving person from consequences communicates several unhealthy messages. For instance, grace manipulators communicate that the family is more concerned with comfort than with dignity and character. They also communicate satisfaction with and acceptance of immature behavior (Kimmel, 2004). In grace-manipulating families, relationship without rules leads to running wild. The recipients of such lazy grace ultimately lose the freedom to choose and the opportunity to learn from the consequences of their choices.

Grace Receivers

Grace receivers learn to combine grace with discipline. They realize that we all sin and they willingly struggle with sin together. Gracious families discipline misbehavior in order to bring it into the light of Christ and help the person grow closer to God, promoting a Christ-like character. They also offer a structure that helps to promote appropriate behavior as part of their discipline. Grace receivers offer an instructive grace.

Grace receivers build healthy relationships that communicate unconditional acceptance as the starting point for effective discipline. They realize that effective discipline, with the goal of self-control and godly character, flows from secure loving relationships. Relationship studies support this idea, revealing that those who experience a secure relationship within the family are better behaved, more independent, and exhibit more empathy and love toward others.

Family members have to spend time together to develop secure relationships. They have to be available, attentive, and responsive. Gracious families intentionally build in family times to help make this possible. Family meals and family activities become opportunities to share their lives, offer support, and build relationships. These relational activities become opportunities to "train in self-control, character, or orderliness and efficiency" (Webster, 1980).

Gracious families also take advantage of both spontaneous and structured transition moments to build relationships. Spontaneous transition moments might include driving a family member to some activity or inviting a family member to "run some errands" with you. Whereas grace rejecters become frustrated when they have to interrupt their busy schedule to manage these spontaneous moments, grace receivers recognize such moments as opportunities to build more intimate relationships. They give greater priority to the relationship than to the busy schedule and gladly seize on opportunities to spend even a little bit of time developing the family relationships that undergird effective discipline.

Structured transition moments include those transitions that naturally occur on a daily basis such as getting up in the morning, preparing for bed, leaving for work or school, returning home from work or school, and preparing meals. Available, attentive, and responsive families utilize these transitions to touch base, review the day, and build intimacy.

Getting up in the morning can set the mood for the whole day. Loving interactions while getting up and preparing to leave for work or school primes us for a more positive and productive day. Days tend to go better when we start them with loving interactions. I used to love visiting my grandparents' home. I slept on the couch in the living room, adjacent to the kitchen. Each morning I would wake up to hear my grandparents quietly discussing their morning devotion and the plans for the day. Their quiet morning conversations filled me with a sense of peace and calm, a realization of my secure place in a loving family.

Taking time to touch base upon returning home can help relieve the stress of work or school and allow family members to debrief, comfortably entering the soothing family space of home. Making time for this transition allows family members to share exciting news, frustrating interactions, and typical events that occur throughout the day. Doing so builds emotional connectedness and intimate relationships.

Preparing for meals also offers a wonderful time to talk and build relationships. I remember moments of simple conversation with my mother as she finished preparing dinner and I set the table. Although these conversations were brief and I cannot recall the actual content of the conversations, I remember the moments with fondness and a sense of security.

Many families have talked about bedtime as an exceptional time to talk. There seems to be something about the end of the day that opens people (both young and old) to intimate communication. Taking the time to talk as a family member prepares for bed provides an opportunity to review the day, resolve unspoken hurts and fears, and verbalize words of appreciation and thanks.

Each of these transition moments teaches us to schedule our lives in a healthy way that promotes relationships and growth. Family members learn to discipline their schedule and their interactions as they experience the structure these transition moments provide. Grace receivers intentionally utilize such moments to teach self-control and provide a secure backdrop for developing godly character.

Grace Receivers and Consequences

Of course, grace receivers do not stop with mere acceptance and personal availability during daily routines. They also allow family members to experience the consequences of their behavior. Grace receivers realize that not allowing a person to experience the consequences of her own behavior actually shows a lack of love and grace. They love one another too much to protect one another from the negative consequences of inappropriate behavior or to rob one another of the positive consequences of appropriate behavior.

Allowing the consequences of behavior teaches wisdom. Through the experience of consequences, family members learn that inappropriate behavior produces more long-term discomfort than appropriate behavior. They learn how to look ahead and consider possible consequences when making wise choices. Not allowing a person to experience the natural and logical consequences of a chosen course of action actually robs the family member of the opportunity to grow in wisdom and the freedom to learn wisdom.

Protecting someone from the consequences of behavior also communicates several dangerous messages. First, it communicates a lack of respect for the person, implying that he is incapable of learning from the consequences or too weak to manage them.

Second, protecting a person from the consequences of behavior communicates that we place a higher priority on keeping people comfortable than on promoting personal dignity and maturity. Sometimes promoting dignity and mature behavior necessitates making the hard and difficult choice, which may produce some short-term discomfort.

Third, protecting family members from the consequences of their behavior communicates that what we say does not have to match what we do. When we constantly talk about how wrong something is but protect the person from the consequences of that wrong action, we send a mixed message. Which message is more accurate? Which is most "listened" to? Of course, actions speak louder than words.

Finally, protecting family members from the discomfort and pain of inappropriate behavior expresses a lack of love. People may protect family members from consequences because they do not want to see them suffer. It is selfish to prevent consequences because "I" do not like to see them suffer. In so doing, the "protective" person selfishly places his own short-term desire (to not see them suffer) above the other person's long-term need (maturity). Selfishly seeking one's own needs at the expense of the other person's needs is tantamount to a lack of love.

Family members may also avoid giving consequences because they do not want to invest the time and energy necessary to enforce the consequence. Not investing time and energy in another person expresses a lack of love. Remember, the currency of love is time and emotional connection. Love is spelled T-I-M-E (McDowell, 2000).

Loving Not Crushing

Grace receivers do not crush one another with consequences; they love one another with consequences. Consider these important aspects about consequences received in grace-receiving families:

- Grace receivers view discipline from a long-term perspective. They consider discipline a way to promote long-term growth and maturation. Grace receivers also realize that discipline promotes intimacy over the long-term even though it may create discomfort and frustration in the short-term.

- Grace receivers clearly focus on behaviors rather than on character when offering a consequence. They do not attack the person's character. They separate the behavior from the person. There is no name-calling, demeaning comments, or threats. They focus on behavior instead.

- Grace receivers believe the best about others, even the misbehaving person. Love believes all things, hopes all things, and bears all things even when dealing with misbehavior. Gracious families believe that family members truly do want to grow in maturity. They believe that family members ultimately do want to please the family with whom they have an intimate relationship. They have a deep-seated belief that the person is capable of learning, growing, and maturing.

- Grace receivers empathize with a person's discomfort and pain without protecting them from the consequences of their behavior. They remain available throughout the consequence, allowing the person to experience grace and truth. This involves communicating an understanding of the discomfort of the consequence while maintaining the consequence. Doing this effectively means balancing the hard line of a consequence while at the same time expressing the soft emotion of empathy.

- Grace receivers teach appropriate behavior as part of the discipline process. They begin by evaluating the negative behavior, even considering the impact of the negative behavior on the person and those around him. It is important for all of us to realize the impact of negative behavior on our lives and the lives of those around us. Then grace receivers teach more appropriate behaviors through discussion and problem-solving that takes family values and beliefs into account.

- Grace receivers talk about potential problem situations ahead of time in order to prevent problem behaviors. Once again, these discussions revolve around potential consequences as well as family values and beliefs.

- Grace receivers continue to restore relationships whenever negative behaviors threaten to destroy them. They follow consequences with a reassurance of love for the person.

14 A PLAYFUL GOD

"You can discover more about a person in an hour of play than in a year of conversation."

–Plato (quoted on nifplay.org)

"It [play] energizes us and enlivens us. It eases our burdens. It renews our natural sense of optimism and opens us up to new possibilities."

–Stuart Brown, MD

"The Son of Man came eating and drinking, and they say, 'Behold a gluttonous man and a drunkard, a friend of tax-gatherers and sinners!' Yet wisdom is vindicated by her deeds."

–Matthew 11:19

Does our Heavenly Father play? Does He celebrate with His family, His children? Earthly fathers bond with their children through play. They offer challenges and instill confidence in their children through play. God is our Heavenly Father. He definitely offers us the challenge of following Christ, of daily taking up our cross and following Him. But does He engage in play with us?

Mothers also bond with their children through play. They bounce their children on their knee while playing "peek-a-boo" or run a "tickling pair of fingers" over their stomach. They bond and nurture through play. God is the One who comforts us like a mother, provides us with nourishment, carries us on His hip, and rests us on his knees (Isaiah 66:12-13). Does God play with His children as a mother plays with her children? Does God nurture, bond, challenge, and instill confidence in His children through play?

One day while cutting the grass, I quietly contemplated the idea of God's playfulness. I do a lot of thinking while cutting grass. Anyway, as I was cutting the grass deep in thought about God and play, a deer came from behind me and nudged my shoulder. I know deer cut though our yard all the time, usually at dusk or dawn. I have seen the evidence of them bedding down in our yard, and, unfortunately, I have seen the evidence of their eating habits in my garden. But I have never had a deer nuzzle my shoulder. I froze. I did not want to startle the deer and have him attack me, so I stood very still for a second and looked out of the corner of my eye. I could not see anything. Very slowly, cautiously, I turned to look at the deer. Then I saw it…a low-hanging tree branch that had snagged my collar. Immediately, I had the impression of God laughing and saying, "Gotcha!" I started to laugh. Maybe God does play. He certainly was messing with me that day.

Interestingly, Scripture has a word for play—*sachaq*. The Hebrew word *sachaq* occurs 36 times in the Old Testament. Zechariah talks about a city "filled with boys and girls *playing (sachaq)* in its streets" (Zechariah 8:5). *Sachaq* can also refer to "laughing at" someone the way God laughs at those who try to gather against Him (Psalm 2:4) or those who plot against the righteous (Psalm 37:13). Other times *sachaq* refers to celebrating, with or without playing instruments, as David did when he brought the Ark of the Covenant back to Jerusalem. He and "all the house of Israel were *celebrating (sachaq)* before the Lord with all kinds of instruments" (2 Samuel 6:5). When Michal complained about David's dancing, he replied that he would "*celebrate (sachaq)* before the Lord" because of all God had done for him (2 Samuel 6:21; 1 Chronicles 15:29). In still other passages, *sachaq* is translated "rejoicing" as in Proverbs 8:30-31: "Then I was beside Him as a master workman; and I was daily His delight, *rejoicing (sachaq)* always before Him, *rejoicing (sachaq)* in the world, His earth, and having my delight in the sons of men."

God does play. He rejoices in His creation. He delights in the sons of men. He encourages celebration and the making of a "joyful noise" (Psalm 95:1; 98:4-6; 100). If we want our families to shine forth the glory of God, we need to emulate His playfulness and celebration. In fact, playful, celebratory interaction with God, His creation, and one another is an integral part of the intentional Christian family.

Celebrating Creation

"In the beginning God created…." I like to think of creation as a family project, Father and Son working together to create all things. We know that God created the heavens and the earth through Jesus (Genesis 1:1; John 1:1-3; Colossians 1:16). The Father and Son worked together to create an extravagant world that exceeds our wildest imaginations. We stand in wonder at the platypus and the giraffe, the dung beetle and the eagle. We watch the slow movement of a snail, the speed of an octopus, and the grace of the hawk. We stand amazed at the colors of a sunset reflecting off Autumn leaves, the grandeur of snow-covered mountains, and the vastness of a clear, starry night. We can experience the soft, oily texture of sheep, the silky texture of a butterfly wing, the rough texture of bark, or the sharp edge on a blade of grass. We enjoy the sweet aroma of oranges and turn from the putrid stench of rotting apples. We can hear the sound of crickets at night, mourning doves at dawn, the purr of a kitten, the howl of the wind, or the ferocious roar of the lion. We have felt the refreshing rain on our faces, witnessed the overwhelming power of a tsunami, and basked in the sun on the beach. God's creation is vast, amazing, and extravagant.

When God first completed His creation, He "saw all that He had made, and behold, it was very good" (Genesis 1:31). Proverbs 8 expands on God's response to His creation. The writer of Proverbs tells his readers that the Wisdom of God (also the description of Christ in 1 Corinthians 1:24) was rejoicing *(sachaq)* before God, rejoicing *(sachaq)* in God's creation, and having His delight in the sons of men (Proverbs 8:30-31). Think about those verses. Wisdom was always before God, playing with creation and taking great delight in men. Like a loving Father, God enjoyed watching Wisdom playfully celebrate His creation.

I love to read how God describes His creation to Job (Job chapters 38-41). He speaks with obvious delight as He describes "commanding the morning," "walking the recesses of the deep," leading forth constellations, and walking through the storehouses of hail and snow (Job 38). I can imagine the adoration in His voice as He describes the Behemoth (Job 40:15-24) and the Leviathan (Job 41).

The psalmist also describes God's amazing creation in Psalm 104. In verses 25-26 the psalmist mentions the Leviathan that God formed to "sport" in the sea. The word for "sport" is *sachaq*, play. God created the Leviathan to play in the sea. He created the Leviathan so He could enjoy watching it play. Perhaps He enjoys watching the otters play in the rivers, the hawks play on the wind, the fish play in the stream, and the porpoises play in the waves. He surely loves to watch fawns and foals frolicking in the fields and wolf cubs playing in the den. God loves His creation. It is "very good" and He playfully celebrates His creation.

Of course, His favorite creations, the masterpiece in which He takes the greatest care and pride, are the sons of men. He takes great "delight" in the sons of men (Proverbs 8:31). He loves to interact with us and watch us. Like a loving Father, God enjoys watching us play and celebrate all that He has given us. He delights in our energetic, abandoned celebration of His extravagant creation and His gift of life.

The intentional Christian family knows that this playful celebration of God and His creation expands our appreciation and knowledge of the world He has created for us as well as our knowledge of God Himself. If Plato is correct in stating that we "discover more about a person in an hour of play than in a year of conversation," imagine how much we can discover about God in playfully celebrating His creation when we go to the zoo, pick flowers, roll in the grass, make snowmen, play in a stream, or float in a lake.

God loves to see His children, our families, expressing delight in His creation, enjoying His gift with energetic abandon and joy. God and His Wisdom serve as our example for playfully celebrating His creation as a family.

Celebrating Our Salvation

Jesus lived a life marked by celebration. His birth was announced to shepherds with a heavenly choir proclaiming "good news of great joy which shall be for all the people" (Luke 2:10). He began His public ministry by announcing release for captives, recovery of sight for the blind, and liberation for the downcast (Luke 4:18-21). Surely those are words for celebration. Jesus' first miracle occurred at a celebration of love, a wedding in which the participants most likely danced and sang to celebrate the loving union of a man and woman (John 2:1-11). Even Jesus' last supper was a solemn celebration of the redemptive value of His life and blood.

Jesus also spoke of celebration in many of His parables. Look particularly at Luke 15 which records three of Jesus' parables. Each parable speaks of finding something lost. The first one tells of a shepherd who lost a sheep. He searched for that lost sheep until he found it. What did he do next? "He calls together his friends and his neighbors, saying to them, 'Rejoice with me, for I have found my sheep which was lost!'" (Luke 15:6).

The second parable tells of a woman who lost a coin. Like the shepherd, she made a diligent search to find what was lost—the coin. When she finds it she "calls together her friends and neighbors saying, 'Rejoice with me, for I have found the coin which I had lost!'" (Luke 15:9).

The third parable, perhaps the best-known of the three, tells of a prodigal son who demanded his inheritance and then took it and left home and squandered it all on sinful living. After he "hit bottom," he decided to return home to his father. Rather than berate his son, the father rejoiced. He dressed his son in his best robe and gave him a ring and new shoes. He dressed him as one of the family again. He killed a fattened calf and invited his neighbors over to celebrate his son's return. This father celebrated because his son "was dead, and has come to life again; he was lost, and has been found" (Luke 15:24). In response, the neighbors gathered and "began to be merry" (Luke 15:24).

Of course, the prodigal son's older brother heard the "music and dancing" and was offended. He became angry that his father celebrated his wasteful younger brother's return. Notice the father's reply: "We had to be merry and rejoice for this brother of yours was dead and has begun to live, and was lost and has been found" (Luke 15:32). In the Latin Bible, the word for "merry and rejoice" is the same word used to translate *sachaq* in the Latin Old Testament. In other words, the father said, "We had to playfully celebrate your brother's return" (Jacob, 2000).

Salvation brings joy to heaven, an angelic celebration, a festive, playful, and extravagant celebration of joy initiated by God Himself. God does play and celebrate…every time one of His children comes home. Once again, the intentional Christian family can follow Heaven's example by celebrating the gift of salvation and each person who accepts that gift. Intentional Christian families can celebrate every step a person takes closer to Christ and our eternal home. When doing so, our homes become part of the Heavenly celebration, a playful refuge of joy.

Chosen by God

David gave us another example of playful celebration before God. In 2 Samuel 6, David began to move the Ark of the Covenant back to Jerusalem. But he did not follow God's command for carrying the ark. Rather than carrying it with rods as intended by God's design, he moved it on a cart. On the way, the Ark began to fall off the cart and one of the escorts reached out to steady it. As soon as he touched the ark, he died. David became frightened and left the ark at Obed-edom's house.

After some time, David decided to bring the Ark the rest of the way to Jerusalem. This time, he intentionally carried it according to God's design. In addition, David celebrated before God every step of the way. He stopped to offer sacrifice to God every six steps. He also arranged for singing, dancing, shouting, and instruments to join the celebration. David celebrated with such abandon that he began "leaping and dancing" (2 Samuel 6:16). David's wife saw this celebration and became embarrassed. In her embarrassment, she scolded David for his abandoned celebration. David replied that he would "celebrate before the Lord" regardless of how it made him look (2 Samuel 6:21-22). The Hebrew word for "celebrate" is (you guessed it) *sachaq*, play. David said, "I will play before the Lord."

David playfully celebrated before God because God had chosen Him as ruler over Israel (2 Samuel 6:1). In response to being chosen by God, David engaged in an extravagant, playful celebration. In addition, he playfully celebrated because the presence of God was returning to Jerusalem, the City of David. The presence of God results in extravagant, playful celebration.

If David had reason to engage in extravagant, playful celebration before God, we have even more. David was chosen to be king over Israel. We have been chosen by God to become His children, fellow heirs with Christ. We are children of God. Our brother, Jesus, is the prince and we are His fellow-heirs! What a cause for celebration.

David realized God's presence in the Ark of the Covenant, but he could not carry the Ark with Him wherever he went. It was large and required several men to carry it safely and carefully. We, on the other hand, have the indwelling presence of God with us in the form of the Holy Spirit. Wherever we go, God goes with us. What a reason to throw a party! Jesus is Immanuel, God with us. Christ in us, the "hope of glory" (Colossians 1:27).

You are Rich

An elderly woman at the church I attend taught me about true riches and celebration. Every time she saw me, she asked about each member of my family. She also offered a compliment about each of my daughters every time we spoke. As our conversation would near an end, she would say, "You are truly rich" or "You are so blessed." Every time she said that I smiled. Sometimes my eyes watered as I realized just how richly God had blessed me with my family. Truly, I have done nothing to deserve such blessings. I have not earned the riches of unconditional love and intimate fellowship. None of us does.

What can we do in response to the rich blessings of our spouse and our children? Celebrate! Enjoy their presence. Rejoice in their love. Amazingly, as we engage in the extravagant, playful celebration of our family before God, we learn more about them than we ever could through simple conversation. In play, families meet with defenses down, trusting one another to respond in kind and cooperate in building a safe world together.

Anticipating Celebration

Someday Christ will return and take us home to Heaven. Jeremiah tells us that God will restore His people. When He does, "thanksgiving and the voice of those who make merry" will proceed from His people (Jeremiah 30:19). Those He has restored will take up their "tambourines, and go forth to the dances of the merry makers" (Jeremiah 31:4). Those who "make merry" and the "merry makers" are both *sachaq*. In other words, the restored will playfully celebrate and go to the dances of those who playfully celebrate God's restoration.

When we anticipate God's return and the restoration of a face-to-face eternal relationship with Him, we shout thanksgiving, take up our tambourine, and playfully celebrate. Knowing that we will one day reside with God in Heaven frees us to playfully celebrate with full, child-like abandon.

I love the way Zechariah tells us about the time of God's return.

> "Thus says the Lord, 'I will return to Zion and will dwell in the midst of Jerusalem. Then Jerusalem will be called the City of Truth, and the mountain of the Lord of hosts will be called the Holy Mountain.' Thus says the Lord of hosts, 'Old men and old women will again sit in the streets of Jerusalem, each man with his staff in his hand because of his age. And the streets of the city will be filled with boys and girls playing [*sachaq*] in its streets" (Zechariah 8:3-5).

When God returns and dwells among His people, the city will be a city of Truth and the mountains around it Holy. As God's children we will live in Holiness and Truth enjoying the presence of God. When God returns and truth abounds in a place of true holiness, we will be free from worry. We will be free of any concern about other people's opinions. We will know freedom from sin and temptation. We, like David, will come before our God with unrestrained, playful celebration, taking great delight in His creation and His people, engaging in an extravagant celebration of His presence and His salvation. That is a reason to celebrate!

A Glimpse of Heaven

God has designed the family to offer a glimpse of this heavenly celebration. Within the family we can playfully celebrate all that God has given us in His creation. We can celebrate each family member's unique contribution, those special gifts that God has built into each individual masterpiece. We can celebrate our birth into this life; and, with all the heavenly hosts, we can celebrate each person's birth into eternal life. We can celebrate that God has chosen us not just for His family in Heaven but for the unique family that He has given us on earth.

The family offers a glimpse of heaven, a taste of the eternal banquet God has prepared for us in Heaven, a foretaste of celebration beyond our wildest dreams. As such, the intentional Christian family becomes a place of celebration, laughter, and playfulness as we delight in one another's presence and unique contribution.

As intentional Christian families join together in celebratory play, they discover the true blessing of family. They grow more acquainted with the riches of intimate fellowship, unconditional acceptance, loving support, and unspeakable joy. When family members play together they build a "joyful union" (Brown, 2009), attuning to one another. They become more aware of one another and more willing to reach out to touch one another both on a physical and an emotional level. As families engage in play, time stands still. There is no past or future, only the eternally present moment, a temporary and limited moment of perfection in an imperfect world. In this way, the celebrating community of family offers us a glimpse of Heaven!

15 CELEBRATION AND DISCIPLINE

"I fear no evil, for You are with me; Your rod and your staff, they comfort me."

—Psalm 23:4

"From first to last, the gospel is a joy-producing good news."

—Gary Thomas

"Correct your son and he will give you comfort; He will also delight your soul."

—Proverbs 29:17

I will always remember November 14, 1992, as one of the most joyous days of my life. On that day my wife and I were married. I arrived at the church early because I had nothing to do but anticipate. Although it was a beautiful day, it had rained the previous night and the church roof was leaking cats and dogs. Roofers stomped around up on the roof and down below huge buckets lined the hallways to catch the dripping water. I didn't care; I was getting married. Fortunately, the roofers finished their work and removed the buckets from the hallways long before guests arrived.

Our wedding turned out beautiful (of course, I may be just a wee bit prejudiced). Our friend sang a song. My father performed the ceremony. Our friends and family gathered and supported our decision. My heart skipped a beat when my wife said, "I do." And a smile spread across my face when we sealed our vows with a kiss.

After the pictures, we packed the train of my wife's dress into a car and my brother escorted us to the reception. We had a wonderful time at our wedding reception. Everyone enjoyed good food. Music played and people danced. The sound of laughter and joyous conversation filled the room. Friends and family seemed to smile, hug, kiss, dance…and smile again. I believe our wedding will go down in history as one of the most joyous celebrations ever attended.

I do anticipate another wedding celebration, though, an eternal wedding reception to celebrate the union of Christ and His Bride, the Church. I thoroughly enjoyed the reception celebrating our wedding, but it will pale in comparison to the joy of that final wedding feast in Heaven. As the old hymn says, "What a day of rejoicing it will be!"

Between the wedding feast celebrating my marriage and the eternal wedding feast of Heaven, I have my family. I love my family. I look forward to sharing moments of laughter and play with them. I cherish our celebrations and rejoice in our lives. In fact, my wife and I consciously strive to make our family a glimpse of Heaven, a keyhole view of that eternal wedding reception celebrating the union of Christ and His Bride. When our children leave home, I hope they will not only look back and remember our family as a safe haven of love and care but as a place of joyful celebration and laughter as well.

Paradoxically, the home cannot become a refuge of joyful celebration and laughter without discipline. Families that try to have joy and celebration without discipline end up with chaos and pain instead. Take away discipline and celebration disappears.

On the other hand, families that maintain loving discipline learn to celebrate. Consider the examples of Noah and Jonah.

Sailing With Noah or Jonah

God was so "grieved in His heart" over the wickedness of mankind that He determined to destroy the earth with a flood. Only one man, Noah, had remained faithful to God. And thus, only Noah and his family would escape the flood. God gave Noah specific instructions for building an ark by which he would be saved. Noah built the ark according to God's specifications, using only the materials that God designated. He filled the ark with animals and foods just as God had ordered. Then, when God called for boarding, Noah and his family boarded the ark and God sealed the door behind them.

As Noah and his family entered the ark, the rain fell and great flood waters began to rise. In the ark, Noah and his family remained safe throughout the flood. I am sure that they had some frightening moments, but they remained safely on the ark until the flood waters receded. Then Noah and his family safely left the ark and began a new life under God's covenant sign of a rainbow (Genesis 7-9). Noah's disciplined obedience to God, and his family's disciplined obedience to his reporting of God's instructions, led them to safety, security, and, ultimately, to celebration.

Compare Noah's story with the story of Jonah, a prophet of God. God told Jonah to sail to the city of Nineveh and call the Ninevites to repentance. Jonah, of course, did not want to tell the hated Ninevites to repent. So he set sail for Tarshish, away from "the presence of the Lord." On the way to Tarshish the ship sailed into a storm so violent and fierce that the ship's captain feared that his ship would break apart in the wind and waves. The crew worked under the captain's orders to secure the ship and save their lives. The captain and crew soon realized, however, that the storm was too great and their efforts too ineffective to save the ship. They called everyone on board to a common area and drew lots in an effort to discover why the storm had fallen upon them.

Jonah drew the short straw. All eyes turned to Jonah as he explained that he was running from God. He told the crew to throw him overboard to save the ship. Not wanting to throw Jonah into the stormy sea, the crew members tried their best to sail and row through the storm—but to no avail. Eventually, they gave in to Jonah's advice and threw him into the sea. When they did, two things happened. First, the storm died down and the sea became calm. Second, a great fish swallowed Jonah. For three days and three nights Jonah prayed from within the belly of that fish. Then the fish vomited Jonah onto the shore.

Life on the Ship

So with whom would you rather sail—Noah or Jonah? To be honest you would have experienced trials and storms on either ship. Both ships were tossed about by the awesome power of the storm and the resultant waves. The crew on the ship with Jonah, however, experienced fear and terror as Jonah attempted to run from God. The ship lost its cargo and one passenger (Jonah). The crew had to carry out the torturous task of throwing Jonah overboard and watching him sink into the sea before a giant fish made a meal of him.

On the ship with Noah, on the other hand, the passengers knew they were safe in God's hand. They lost no passengers and no cargo and in time safely came to ground. After arriving at their God-given destination safe and sound, they remained on the ship until God revealed that it was safe to disembark. When they left the ship, they immediately worshipped God under His rainbow.

So let me ask once again: With whom would you rather sail—Noah or Jonah? The choices that both men made impacted everyone around them. The consequences of their choices affected the whole community with whom they sailed. Noah responded to God with disciplined obedience and those on the ship with him were secure in the hand of God. Jonah, on the other hand, responded to God with undisciplined disobedience and ran from God. He was determined to seek his own way and act according to his own will, not God's. As a result, those on the ship with him feared for their lives and were left no choice but to throw a ship mate into a stormy sea.

The principle remains every bit as true today as it was in the days of Noah and of Jonah. We cannot make someone live or think a particular way. God endowed each of us with free will, to act as we choose. Nor can we blame other people for our choices. Our lives do impact the lives of those in our family, however, just as their lives impact us. We are sailing on a ship with our family. Each person's life—including the choices he or she makes—impacts the whole. Does your family sail with Noah or Jonah?

Sailing with Jonah

Families that set sail without discipline have boarded ship and sail with Jonah. By avoiding discipline, they disobey God's command to discipline. Like Jonah, they set sail on a course away from the presence of God, determined to make their own way. And just like Jonah they soon find themselves sailing in a storm of chaos and pain.

Some families avoid discipline because they know it will bring momentary pain and suffering. Like Jonah, they fear that obedient discipline might alter relationships. Unlike Jonah, they fear that discipline will make the disciplined family member feel bad. Fearing that the pain of discipline will create momentary sorrow, they do not teach obedience or encourage character. So, to avoid momentary painful consequences, they avoid discipline. Ironically, their efforts to keep the peace—and "not make waves"—lead them to became lost in a storm of permissiveness.

In a permissive environment, family members become self-centered. They begin to think only of themselves, putting their own needs and desires above other family members' needs and desires.

Family members also develop a sense of entitlement. People who feel a sense of entitlement become demanding. They do not believe that they have to work for or earn anything; they are entitled to rewards, to whatever they want, in fact. Rather than focus on other people, they selfishly demand that other people cater to their own desires. Self-centeredness, entitlement, and demands devastate any sense of community and rob the family of celebration.

Eventually, families that avoid discipline will experience frustration and regret. Individual family members develop self-loathing while the whole family suffers the consequences of "falling apart." They struggle in a storm of stress. If only one person is causing the chaos, the family struggles with the decision of whether or not to throw the undisciplined member overboard. They do everything possible to keep that family member close (such as excusing, enabling, and bailing him out), even to the point of losing cargo and supplies along the way. Families willingly give up everything in their effort to save another family member from his or her own poor choices. Sometimes the prodigal recognizes this sacrifice and returns. Sometimes he does not. Either way, family members experience the ill effects of stress on their physical and emotional health.

Winds of fear and self-doubt toss family members about as they ponder what, if anything, they have done to contribute to or even cause the problem. Waves of loneliness and regret beat on the family. Sharp rocks of frustration rise up under the hull and threaten to break the family apart. The sense of community diminishes. Family members struggle to keep the family ship afloat. In the midst of this storm, there is no time or opportunity to celebrate.

Wisdom from Noah

Noah, on the other hand, understood that disciplined obedience and a disciplined life would lead to security, even in the midst of a storm. He recognized that only disciplined obedience would allow his family to remain together. So, when God called him to build an ark, he did so, and even involved his whole family in the project.

Imagine what it might have been like for Noah and his family as they built the ark. They had never built an ark or even a row boat, for that matter. They did not even have a large body of water in which to sail a boat. The only way they knew what to do—their only hope of success—was through God's instructions. They had to follow those instructions to the letter or the ark might sink. As a result, the whole family must have listened very carefully to Noah as he repeated God's instructions for building the ark. They must have remained open to his wise correction when they strayed from God's instruction. This atmosphere of discipline involved careful listening, wise words of correction, and humble acceptance of those words so that the ark could be built to God's exact specifications.

Eventually, this atmosphere of discipline led to the celebration of life, God's love, and deliverance.

I imagine that Noah's neighbors ridiculed and teased him as he spent 120 years building an ark. Noah may have used this opportunity to teach and warn the neighbors. Perhaps he proclaimed God's judgment and pleaded with them to repent of their sin. I am sure that he held his family and friends accountable to the word of God. His family accepted this discipline and eventually celebrated together. His neighbors rejected the discipline and found themselves in the rising waters of God's wrath.

Noah must have taken great delight in watching his own sons and their wives working with him on the ark. He must have felt delight in his having family working together, available to one another and to the call of God, accountable and obedient to the command of God. I have no doubt that Noah and his family made great sacrifices as they built the ark. Disciplined obedience to God cost them friendships. It shaped how they interacted with one another. It also allowed them to celebrate as a family. Disciplined obedience to God allowed them to survive the flood as a family and worship God as a family after the storm ended. Discipline allowed for, and led to, celebration.

The Celebration of Discipline

A family of celebration realizes that "all discipline for the moment seems not to be joyful, but sorrowful; yet to those who have been trained by it, afterwards, it yields the peaceful fruit of righteousness" (Hebrews 12:11). To promote a truly celebrating community, the family must have discipline.

A community of celebration demands that family members think of others and not just of themselves. Discipline teaches us that we do not exist in a vacuum. It teaches us that our behavior and choices impact those around us. Through discipline we remain aware of how our behavior affects those around us and teaches us to respect and honor them. In honor we can then alter our behavior appropriately.

As family members learn to remain aware of one another and respond to one another in love and honor, the family becomes a safe haven, a safe ship in which to travel. The safe haven that discipline creates provides many other benefits as well. For instance, a sense of safety and security opens the door to intimacy. Family members who feel safe can open up and become vulnerable, trusting that the family will nurture and protect them. Greater intimacy leads to greater confidence among individual family members. In fact, loving discipline is built on the mutual respect that contributes to individual confidence. Greater intimacy also leads to greater obedience and less defiance.

A family that practices loving discipline will more likely experience a sense of community as well. Individual family members develop a greater level of self-discipline. In an atmosphere of acceptance, families will have a greater sense of peace and be more likely to practice mutual honor in the midst of any disagreements that arise. As this acceptance grows, so does individual character and self-acceptance. Overall, discipline helps create a family environment conducive to celebration.

Family members do have to learn to graciously teach one another to live godly and in harmony with one another, gently confronting sin and behaviors that interfere with family life. They need to humbly listen to one another and adjust their behavior accordingly. Discipline within the family teaches us to do this.

Most of us do not naturally make our own needs secondary to other people's needs. We do not naturally confront sin in a loving manner or humbly listen as other people confront our sin. We have to learn how to live out these godly actions. Family offers the optimal environment in which we can learn these disciplines. At times, this learning process is difficult, yes, but the long-term benefits far outweigh any temporary pain or discomfort or growing pains we might experience.

Summary

Although discipline can be painful for the moment, it gives strength and stability in the storm and lays the foundation for celebration. Let me briefly review the key points explaining how discipline contributes to celebration.

1. Discipline teaches us to think of others as more important than ourselves (Philippians 2:3) and to value one another as God's masterpiece.

2. Discipline teaches us to remain aware of those around us and concerned for their safety and health. With this awareness, family members can modify their behavior for the benefit of the family rather than for selfish reasons.

3. Family members learn to humbly listen to and acknowledge one another through discipline. Listening and acknowledging one another shows mutual respect and allows family members

to adjust their behavior accordingly. Mutual respect leads to greater individual confidence.

4. Learning to respectfully listen to other family members leads to a greater awareness of one another. A greater awareness of our fellow family members enables us to know what pleases them and communicates love to them. In this way, awareness and listening leads to greater intimacy and relational security. Loving discipline makes this possible.

5. Discipline also involves looking out for one another's welfare. We do this by gently holding one another accountable and offering loving correction. At the same time, we need to offer loving correction with an attitude of respect, humility, and love, addressing the "plank in our own eye" as well.

6. Discipline also teaches us to accept loving correction and accountability. Family members internalize family values in this atmosphere and become more self-disciplined as a result.

7. Discipline teaches family members to protect one another and to celebrate one another. The family of loving, gentle discipline develops a safe haven of love and celebration that encourages playful interaction based on mutual respect.

Overall, the family that practices discipline survives the storms and ultimately celebrates under the rainbow of God's love and discipline.

16 RITUALS OF CONNECTION

. . . .

"The truly great advances of this generation will be made by those who can make outrageous connections, and only a mind which knows how to play can do that."

—Nagle Jackson (quoted on nifplay.org)

"I will rejoice over them to do them good."

—Nehemiah 30:41

The Father Rejoices

I love God's word to His family through Zephaniah. He tells His children that the day is coming in which "the Lord your God is in your midst, a victorious warrior. He will exult over you with joy, He will be quiet in his love, He will rejoice over you with shouts of joy" (Zephaniah 3:17). What a celebration in which even God will shout for joy over His children's coming home.

When I read this verse, I remember the births of our children. I have two daughters, and each birth filled me with so much joy and happiness that I could hardly contain myself. I held them in my arms and looked into their eyes, exulting over them with an overwhelming joy. I looked from them to my wife and felt even greater love and adoration. Together, we rejoiced in each daughter's precious new life. There were no words to express our joy and love. Quietly, we watched one another in a silent celebration of love and life. But when I left the hospital my quiet celebration turned into singing and shouting and exuberant dancing. I turned on the radio and sang along...*loudly!*

That is how God feels about His children when they come home. He can hardly contain His joy when He looks into our eyes and shares a loving gaze. He gazes into our lives with an overwhelming joy, quietly celebrating our life in Him and the intimacy we will share with Him for eternity. But that quiet love gives way to the noise of celebration—singing, dancing, shouting, and making merry. A heavenly celebration of family, intimacy, and abundant life.

The intentional Christian family gives us a foretaste of this joyful celebration. Creating this type of family takes intentional effort. Without intentional effort, the world will lead our family toward entropy (Doherty, 1997). We will experience growing distance and isolation. Each family member will go his own way and become involved in his own life. We will find ourselves cocooned in our individual rooms watching our own TV, playing our own game, and listening to our own music. We may find ourselves walking together while listening to our own music in our own ear phones or talking on our own phones carrying on conversations with other people—physically in proximity but emotionally and mentally worlds apart.

One way to avoid entropy and intentionally build intimacy is to create rituals in the family. Rituals are the glue that holds a family together. They celebrate family, intimacy, and life. Family rituals do several things to help us build intimacy.

- First, rituals build connection. Successful rituals require everyone's involvement and cooperation.

- Second, rituals build predictability and anticipation. They give family members something to look forward to, an anticipation of enjoyable family time. Because rituals are repeated, family members anticipate the next occurrence and can plan their schedules around the ritual. The anticipation of a fun ritual leads to family members' making the intentional effort to spend time together.

- Third, family rituals build family identity. We become the family of "campers," "fun-loving game players," "church participants," "volunteers," or any other identifying marker your family may enjoy.

- Fourth, rituals help us instill our values into each family member. We put what we believe into practice. We celebrate the shared meaning of our family through rituals.

Our Example

Jesus established one of the most well-known rituals for the church family when He instituted the Lord's Supper. During Passover, a celebratory ritual recalling God's deliverance, Jesus took some bread, gave thanks for it, broke it, and passed it out to His disciples saying, "This is My body, broken for you; do this in remembrance of me." Then, He took a cup of wine, gave thanks for it, and passed it to His disciples saying, "This cup is the new covenant in My blood; do this, as often as you drink it, in remembrance of me. For as often as you eat this bread and drink the cup, you proclaim the Lord's death until He comes" (1 Corinthians 11:23-26). With those actions and words Jesus established one of the most well-known Christian rituals, a ritual that celebrates Christ's willingness to sacrifice for us and calls to mind the future hope of eternal life.

Take a moment to consider the Lord's Supper as a powerful, intentional ritual that Christ established for His family. First, Jesus involves the disciples in the Lord's Supper to build a connection with them. He also deepens His personal connection with us each time we share in Communion. In addition, the Lord's Supper builds connections among God's children around the world. It marks us as members of His family. God's family joins together in communion to celebrate the work of Christ, connecting in a deep and mysterious way as His Body and Bride.

Second, those in the family of God participate in Communion on a regular basis. The church I attend celebrates communion each week. Other churches celebrate monthly. Either way, God's family anticipates sharing in this memorial meal, arranging schedules so as to not miss the opportunity to grow closer to Christ and His Church through the sharing of the Lord's Supper.

Jesus also built anticipation into the Lord's Supper when He said that He would not partake again until in "His Father's Kingdom" (Matthew 26:26-29) and that continuing the Lord's Supper proclaims His death "until He comes" (1 Corinthians 11:23-26). Each time I share in the Lord's Supper I anticipate Christ's return and the joy of sharing this ritual with Him face-to-face in the future.

Third, sharing the Lord's Supper establishes our identity as Christians, children of God. It reminds us of the price God paid to bring us into His family and identify us with Christ. Recalling the price of God's love for His children brings us to the fourth aspect of this ritual.

Fourth, the ritual of the Lord's Supper brings to mind our Christian values of sacrifice, humility, obedience, trust, unity, and joy. We recall these values as we contemplate Christ's act of sacrificing Himself on the cross for us while we were yet undeserving of such love. We remember that He calls us to live by the same values that He lived and died by while in the form of a man.

Jesus instituted the Lord's Supper as a mysterious and perfect ritual with deep meaning and purpose. This ritual has existed for over 2,000 years and has never grown old. It requires each Christian's participation, builds predictability and anticipation, confirms us in our identity, and instills Christian values in our hearts and minds. Although our own rituals may not prove as perfect as His, they can accomplish similar goals within our family.

A Rituals Primer

We can create many types of rituals in our family, but all the rituals will share several key factors. First, whatever the ritual, simple or complex, the goal is to build relationships and greater intimacy.

Second, rituals take time. In order for a ritual to prove successful, we have to create the space for it. We cannot complete a ritual in a rush. We have to slow down and spend time enjoying the ritual. Each ritual requires that we make time for a beginning, a body, and an ending. The beginning of a ritual carves out the time needed to transition from daily activities into the actual body of the ritual. The body of the ritual represents the time we actually spend engaged in the ritual itself. Finally, the ending allows us to exit from the ritual and return to our daily life. A successful ritual will include all three parts—beginning, body, and end.

Third, rituals serve an important function within the family. Children, in particular, come to value the predictability of the ritual and the family time inherent in the ritual. Although parents may initiate a ritual, children often encourage and remind the family to continue it. I recall starting a devotional time with my children, a simple activity that lasted about 10 minutes and was followed by reading a related Bible verse. The activity was usually fun. One week we did not have time for our devotion. My children reminded me the next week, "When is our Bible study, Dad?" As they grew older, those Bible Studies evolved into more private studies. To this day, we have talks about what each of us is learning in our individual and church studies.

We also have a ritual of making Easter cookies on the Saturday night before Easter. The cookies are very simple. The ingredients represent various aspects of Jesus' betrayal, arrest, crucifixion, and resurrection.

One year, my wife and I felt too busy and rushed and decided not to make the cookies. When our daughters asked when we were going to make the cookies, we explained that we had decided not to make them. They insisted that we make the cookies: "We have to, Mom. We *always* do." So, at our children's prompting and request, the ritual continues.

Fourth, rituals may need to be adapted as family members grow and mature. We need to consider the age and personality of family members in relation to the rituals. For instance, bedtime rituals change as children move into their teen years. When children are young, we may spend time reading a book and talking before praying and tucking them into bed. As children become teens, they may not want to read a book together. They may simply pray and go to bed. Eventually, they may even pray on their own at bedtime.

In our family we have a "Dad night" each week. On this night, my wife works and I have the opportunity to spend time with my daughters. When they were young we had a devotional time before eating supper and watching a movie. As they moved into their teen years their schedules began to change. They became involved in various after-school activities, church youth group activities, and music lessons. Though we still had Tuesday evenings together, we often did not have time for the same activities. As a result, we had to modify our ritual. Although the ritual changed as my daughters grew, we continue to spend Tuesday evenings talking about their lives and enjoying one another's company.

What kind of rituals do you have in place in your family? How can you establish more rituals and what rituals might you establish? Consider what activities and routines you already engage in on a daily basis. These activities and routines can form the basis of several meaningful rituals.

Rise and Shine or Off to Bed

Two great times to establish rituals of connection are when you are getting up in the morning and going to bed at night. Establishing a morning ritual allows the family to set the mood for the day and prime the day in a positive direction. Morning rituals include how you wake up in the morning and prepare for the day, what types of interactions you have over breakfast, and how you say good-bye as each family member leaves the home for her daily activities.

Each family has to take into consideration the personality of the family members when establishing a morning ritual. Some people are not "morning people," and the morning ritual may remain very simple as a result. Even a simple morning ritual offers an excellent opportunity to start the day on a positive note.

When our youngest daughter was preschool age, she had difficulty getting everything done to prepare for the day. In our efforts to get her to brush her teeth, comb her hair, put on her clothes, and make her bed we would end up arguing with her. Not a good way to start the day. So we turned the morning into a ritual of connection.

First, we thought about what our daughter liked that might prove motivating. We knew she liked *Dragon Tales.* So we printed a picture of a dinosaur from the show and cut it into puzzle pieces, one piece for each task she needed to complete. We gave her one piece of the puzzle for each task she completed. After she completed the puzzle, we talked about the dragon of the day. She loved it. She could not wait to get ready in the morning. That simple ritual turned the morning "drudgery" into a time of enjoyment and connection. Breakfast became a time of happy conversation about the day instead of grumbling about the morning. The morning conflict was transformed into a meaningful, playful ritual that got the day started on a joyful note.

The bedtime ritual is one of the most powerful family rituals as it presents the opportunity to share the final words of the day and one last expression of love before entering the world of dreams. The bedtime ritual thus presents a wonderful opportunity to connect with one another, entrain daily rhythms, make one another feel special, and give one another attention. The goal of the bedtime ritual is to connect with one another, not simply to get everyone to bed. An added benefit of a bedtime ritual is that everyone goes to bed more easily, in a calmer mood, and better prepared for a good night's sleep.

In establishing a bedtime ritual, recall the pattern of rituals. Each ritual has a beginning, a body, and an ending. When considering the beginning of the ritual, how will you transition from daily activities to the bedtime ritual? This may vary from family member to family member. It may include a bath, changing into pajamas, or having a small snack.

What will you do in the body of your bedtime ritual? How will you connect with one another? Families around the world do this in a variety of ways. You might read books to your children, share devotions with your spouse, pray with one another, or share stories. I also like to review the positive and happy events of the day as well as take the time to talk about and resolve any troubling events of the day. This provides an opportunity to apologize, heal disagreements, and restore damaged relationships.

Giving thanks also helps end the day and drift into the world of dreams on a positive note. Doing so also teaches family members to recognize and pay attention to acts of kindnesses, blessings from God, blessings from others, and the things we enjoyed throughout the day.

Finally, how will you end the bedtime ritual? We end the ritual with a kiss and tuck-in. When our children were young, I would lay in bed with them while they fell asleep and then quietly leave. As they grew older, they learned to fall asleep alone and a simple hug and kiss and a sincere "I love you" ended the ritual.

It all sounds simple, doesn't it? And it is, really. It takes up to half an hour from transition to ending. But what an investment! It adds tremendous meaning to family life. Everyone can participate, even if everyone goes to bed at different times. This ritual builds predictability and anticipation. It offers the opportunity for building deeper connection and identity and to reinforce family values through stories and talking about the day's events. A bedtime ritual also allows time for everyone to wind down from the day and move into a peaceful state of mind that improves sleep quality.

Greetings and Leavings

Two other important daily rituals include how we take our leave from one another and how we greet one another when we reunite. Everyday families rise in the morning, get ready for the day, and go their separate way to complete the day's activities. Some family members go to work, some go to school, and some go about the daily task of maintaining the home. Whatever the task, we say our brief good-byes and go on our way. The daily occurrence of going our separate ways for a time offers the opportunity to build a ritual of connection. Rather than simply running out the door in a last-minute rush, take the time to share your plans for the day. We can listen to one another's plans as well as hopes and fears for the day. Express feelings of love to affirm your bond during the absence. End the ritual with a hug and a kiss. A simple parting has been transformed into a sacred moment of sharing our lives and expressing intimacy.

Reuniting at the end of the day also provides an opportunity to create a ritual of connection. Rather than running into the home and hurrying off to engage in private affairs, take the time to greet one another. Share a kiss. Many marriage counselors have recommended spending several seconds giving your spouse a truly intimate kiss upon returning home from work or daily activities. After the kiss, share a moment of quiet conversation. Talk about the successes and frustrations of the day. Offer one another support and encouragement. Offer assistance when appropriate.

Some people may need to build a transition phase into this ritual, a short time of relaxing alone before greeting the family. I know people who come home from work and prefer 15-20 minutes of quiet time to transition from work to home before greeting their family with a hug, a kiss, and a discussion of the day. Remember, we have to individualize our ritual to our particular families and the unique personalities of our family members.

Mealtime

Our society is so busy that many families do not take the time to enjoy family meals together. Family meals, however, provide an excellent opportunity to connect with one another, build intimacy, and share our lives. Through dinner conversation, families can show and express concern for one another, share victories and frustrations, and refocus on family values while resolving conflicts and minor crises.

Research suggests that sharing meals also reduces the likelihood that children will smoke, drink, or use illegal drugs. Youth who share in family mealtimes are less likely to have sex at young ages and are at a lower risk for thoughts of suicide. Families that share mealtimes also tend to be more emotionally content and have healthier eating habits. Children who have family mealtimes tend to do better in school than those who do not have family meals (http://www.puttingfamilyfirst.org/why_mealtime_is_important.php). Make the investment in family mealtimes as often as possible. The payoff is excellent, not just in the dining experience itself but in your family members' quality of life.

I realize that many things can interfere with family meals—busy schedules, TV, and phone calls, to name just a few. In spite of these interferences, however, intentional Christian families strive to make family meals a priority in their lives. They invest time and effort in making them happen. This may mean that family members put the family dinner on the schedule ahead of time, leave work in order to be home for dinner time, schedule outings with friends at times other than dinner time, let the answering machine pick up the phone during dinner, and turn off the TV.

That said, dinner may not work for your family because of uncontrollable work schedules or other extenuating circumstances. That's OK. Any meal can serve as a *family meal*. If dinner time does not work for your family, you might eat breakfast or lunch as a family instead. Whatever meal works for your family, be sure to eat as a family as many days as you can during the week. Make family meal time a priority.

Make meal times memorable. Have fun. This is probably not the best time or place for dealing with "heavy issues." So try to keep it light and enjoyable. For instance, start your meal with dessert once in awhile. Start the day with pizza and end the day with bacon and eggs. Tell jokes or recall funny stories about family vacations. On special occasions use the good china, light some candles, and roll out the fancy table cloths. On other occasions, have a simple picnic. You might even choose to have an indoor picnic in the middle of winter. Whatever you do, make a point of enjoying one another's company and conversation.

You can also talk about upcoming events, news items of the day, or daily frustrations. Even when speaking about the more "serious matters," though, avoid lecturing and fussing. The point is to bond, so enjoy the conversation and the meal. Create an environment in which the family anticipates the intimate, celebratory conversation of the family mealtime.

Mealtime rituals include more than just sitting down together at the table to eat. Someone has to prepare the meal and set the table. This is part of the transition to mealtime. Involve the whole family or certain family members in the preparation. Preparing meals together provides a wonderful opportunity to develop intimate connections as well as multiple opportunities to learn life skills, nutrition, and even family values. Other benefits are that children can learn some math and how to read and follow directions while enhancing fine motor skills and increasing conversation skills.

Cleaning up is part of ending the ritual and provides the opportunity to honor one another through service. I remember an older couple who attended my church some years ago. The man was a WWII veteran and a retired steel-mill worker. His wife was a retired kindergarten teacher. They invited me to their home for dinner several times. They not only fed me but gave me the privilege of looking at their photo albums. I saw pictures of this tough man in his youth working on the Pacific Islands during WWII. He showed me some "self-defense" moves. Even in his old age he would "wrap me up" before I knew he had even moved. His wife would just smile. She always complimented people. She is one of the kindest people I have ever met and cooked delicious meals as well. After dinner the husband, the WWII veteran and tough steel worker, washed the dishes. I remember smiling as I watched this tough guy wash the dishes. Every time he did, he would look at me and say, "Just remember, if your wife cooks the dinner, you clean it up." It was the ending of the mealtime ritual that they had practiced throughout their marriage—a beautiful ritual of honor, appreciation, and connection.

Family Fun Night

I am not very competitive, but I do enjoy playing with my family. Play is an integral part of human life. It enhances life. It pulls people together and builds our empathy, cooperation, negotiation skills, and impulse control. Play teaches us to manage our emotions better. So it is easy to see why family fun night is such a great ritual.

You may schedule a family fun night once a week or once a month. Do it as often as you like. Here's how. Set the time aside and clear your schedule. Begin the family fun night with a simple meal, such as pizza or hamburgers. Then choose an activity. The activity may vary from night to night. You could play a favorite game, watch a movie, make a craft, have a picnic, go for a walk, go to the zoo, make ice cream, or simply hang out and talk. During the activity, take some pictures. Later, perhaps during a family night, you can put the pictures together in a photo album entitled "Family Nights, 2009." Save the album to review and relive the events as often as you like. It will become a cherished memory book!

Always Remember and Never Forget

We could go on with various ideas for family rituals, but you get the point. The possibilities are limited only by your creativity and desire to have fun as a family. Whatever rituals of connection your family chooses to practice, remember the overall purposes:

1. Enjoy one another's company

2. Share one another's lives

3. Find deeper connections with one another

4. Have fun!

17 RITUALS OF CELEBRATION

· ·

"Celebration is at the heart of the way of Christ."
—Richard Foster

The last chapter focused on rituals of connection. Many rituals of connection occur on a daily or weekly basis. They present opportunities for family members to connect with one another, celebrate relationship, and intentionally draw closer to one another. Rituals of connection provide fertile ground for developing and celebrating our relationships on a regular basis.

This chapter focuses on rituals of celebration. Though rituals of celebration occur less often they still provide the opportunity to connect with one another and to develop intimacy. They also allow us to celebrate each individual, recognizing each family member as special and unique.

Intentional Christian families can utilize many of the special days observed in our society, such as birthdays, Mother's Day, Father's Day, or Children's Day, to create rituals of celebration. With some investment of time and effort we can use these established days to create rituals that celebrate our love and respect for one another without succumbing to the commercial aspects that dilute these celebrations.

Rituals of celebration include rituals of recognition, yearly rituals, rituals of tradition, and rituals that extend beyond the family. While celebrating these rituals, families can spend as little or as much money as they like—that's not the important element. Family members can record the celebrations through pictures, videos, writings, drawings, or any other way they choose. These recorded memories allow families to recall and celebrate their life's story and the unique contributions of each family member.

Rituals of Recognition

Rituals of recognition include events such as birthdays and rites of passage. They celebrate each family member by recognizing his or her inherent value. When we celebrate rituals of recognition we validate each person's unique and significant role in the family.

Birthdays provide an excellent opportunity to recognize individual family members. In preparing for a birthday celebration we recognize the birthday person's unique tastes and personality to honor him or her. Ask the birthday person what would make him or her feel most special. Remember, each family member is different. My daughter enjoys having all of her friends to the house to celebrate. If left to her own devices, we might have 20 people at our house celebrating her birthday. That's not my idea of a special birthday celebration. I enjoy celebrating my birthday with my family over a simple meal while listening to music and talking.

Birthday celebrations will also vary according to personal tastes. In our family we often request special meals for birthdays. I enjoy lasagna. My wife and our daughters enjoy steak and potatoes. Some people like cake and ice cream and others prefer an ice cream cake. Some people even enjoy pie for their birthday or even fresh fruit. Take the time to talk and find out what each person finds most enjoyable on that special day. Let him or her choose the menu, the time of day, and even some of the activities. Doing so honors the person whose "special" day you are observing and makes the celebration special.

Your family may also add unique aspects to the birthday celebration. For instance, some families have a special plate for the birthday person. One family we know has a special hat that the birthday person wears while opening the presents. It's a tall, colorful, cartoonish hat that adults and children alike wear when opening birthday presents. Everyone enjoys seeing the birthday celebrant wearing the hat and everyone takes pictures to share and mark the occasion as special and treasured.

One family I know said they could not sing well and did not like to sing "Happy Birthday." They bought a wind-up toy that played "Happy Birthday" while a ballerina was spinning around. As the wind-up toy plays, they sing along (and, I think, they sound pretty good). They certainly have a good time.

Add some stories to the birthday celebration. Recall funny or adventurous stories that occurred over the last year and share them with one another. Tell the birthday person what you really appreciate about him and support those characteristics with simple stories. They can be funny or sentimental (or both), depending on your family's preference and the overall mood at the time.

In the intentional Christian family we can also celebrate spiritual birthdays. In fact, Jesus said that all of Heaven celebrates when a sinner repents (Luke 15:7, 10). We could join our family with that heavenly celebration by recognizing one another's spiritual birthdays with a card, a dance, a special meal, a party, or a simple "congratulations on eternal life with Christ."

We can recognize one another in similar ways on Mother's Day, Father's Day, and Children's Day. These holidays present wonderful opportunities to tell our family members how much we appreciate them, how valuable they are to the family, and how deeply we love and cherish them.

Rites of Passage

Rites of passage also present opportunities to create rituals of recognition. Rites of passage mark changes in one's abilities or the expectations placed on him as he reaches a new developmental level. Several ages could mark rites of passage in our society. For instance, completing elementary school, completing high school, and completing college all represent significant rites of passage. In addition, becoming a teenager, turning 16, or going on the first date all represent rites of passage. I even know families that found a way to quietly celebrate a woman's first menstrual cycle, recognizing her transition to womanhood. Engagement, marriage, and having children represent other rites of passages that families experience. Perhaps your family also celebrates various religious rites of passage such as confirmation, baptism, or first communion.

Many rites of passage include community celebrations in which the family participates. Unfortunately, many families enjoy the community celebrations (such as a graduation ceremony) but miss out on the individual family celebration. It is important for the intentional Christian family to celebrate various rites of passage as a family as well as with the larger community.

Rites of passage present a unique opportunity to share values and beliefs as well as to validate the individual's core worth. For instance, getting a driver's license presents the opportunity to share lessons about responsibility and concern for others. Moving to college or starting a new job carries the opportunity to share what it means to be a Christian man or woman in a secular world. Getting married presents the opportunity to discuss the values of marriage, commitment, sacrifice, honor, and grace. Having children presents the opportunity to emphasize God as our Father as well as the joys and struggles of attempting to parent "in the image of God." Each rite of passage is ripe with opportunity to share values and beliefs.

During a rite of passage ritual the family may share a special activity to honor the person. This might include a special trip, a dinner, or a gift. Celebrating rites of passage is also an excellent time to bring out the family photo albums or family videos. Whatever activity you choose, take time to tell the person going through the rite of passage what you appreciate and admire about him or her. Reminisce together and share dreams of the future.

I had the opportunity to take each of our daughters on a short backpacking trip during the summer between elementary school and middle school. This trip allowed us to complete a journey that presented a slight physical challenge and gave us some cherished uninterrupted time together. We talked about her positive choices and accomplishments as well as the upcoming school year. We discussed any fears or concerns she might have and her dreams of the future. During this trip, I gave each daughter a verbal blessing in which I acknowledged and admired the positive character traits she exhibited as well as the wise choices she had made thus far in her life. I shared my appreciation and respect for her. I honored her for the courage and wisdom she had shown throughout the first 11 years of her life. I supported each aspect I recognized with specific examples and then encouraged her to continue making the same wise choices. This was done over a period of a couple of days while we had fun, ate, gathered fire wood, watched for deer, climbed rocks, and enjoyed scenic mountain views from various rock outcroppings.

We have had other such rites of passage in our family. We had a special celebration when each daughter turned 13 and plan another when they turn 16. We plan a special family ritual when they graduate from high school. I hope we still celebrate as a family when they graduate from college, get engaged, and get married. As my wife and I strive to develop an intentional Christian family that spans the generations, we hope to find ways of celebrating each rite of passage as they occur. I pray that you will commit to do the same and enjoy the blessings.

Yearly Family Rituals

Vacations are another ritual that may get passed over in our busy world. Vacations allow families an extended period of time together without the usual pressures of work, school, house cleaning, and other mundane daily chores. While vacationing, family members can explore, play, and enjoy one another's company.

At the same time, vacations present unique challenges to the family. Two specific challenges include how to plan the vacation and how to handle concentrated time together.

When planning a vacation, include the whole family. This does not necessitate a formal, sit-down meeting. You can talk about plans while driving to the store or eating dinner as a family. Just take time to dream about the vacation together. Talk about the vacation and available options for activities while listening to discover what arouses special interest in each family member. Talk about activities that each family member might enjoy during the vacation, and schedule some activities in honor of each person. Planning the vacation as a family honors each family member.

Planning and talking about the vacation also builds anticipation and excitement. It helps us transition into the vacation ritual as a family. While on the vacation, talk about future vacations that you might enjoy as a family.

Spending concentrated time together can also lead to some frustrations and irritability. View these as opportunities to problem-solve together based on the values and beliefs of your family. Such problem-solving together can help build intimacy. Also, to help decrease frustrations and irritabilities, coordinate duties, responsibilities, and expectations. Give each family member the *privilege* of participating in the responsibilities involved.

Rituals of Tradition

Traditional holidays also provide a wonderful opportunity to create family rituals. Rituals of tradition such as Christmas, Thanksgiving, and Easter will vary from family to family but all take a common form. First, rituals of tradition include pre-holiday activities—a beginning. To establish a strong holiday ritual, families need to make preparations. Second, rituals of tradition involve a period of engaging in the "main body" of the ritual. Finally, rituals of tradition include an ending that allows the family to leave the ritual space and transition back into ordinary life.

Think about Christmas with me. How does your family prepare for Christmas? What do you do to get into the "Christmas spirit"? Preparation allows our families to slow down and come together as a family instead of being washed downstream by the hustle and bustle of the world and the madness of the "commercialized X-mas."

Buying and decorating a Christmas tree is a ritual many families enjoy in their preparations for Christmas. This "preparatory" ritual allows the family to spend time together. While performing this ritual the family can reminisce about past Christmases, sing carols, listen to Christmas music, and talk about their lives.

A friend told me about a preparatory Christmas ritual that her family has enjoyed. Every year they set up the manger scene early but leave the manger itself empty. In addition, they "hid" the wise men in plain sight somewhere on the other side of the house. Every day, the wise men moved a little closer to the manger. As you can imagine, every day her children went in search of the wise men, excited to see how much closer they had come to the manger. Finally, on Christmas morning the baby Jesus would appear and the wise men would stand within range of the manger scene.

Other Christmas preparations include Advent calendars, Christmas Eve services, preparing and singing Christmas specials, listening to Christmas music, and any other family traditions you have for your Christmas celebration.

Thanksgiving preparations often include buying the turkey, preparing the meal, and sharing blessings and thanks. My family often celebrates Thanksgiving with my wife's sister. As the children have matured, part of our family tradition has grown to include the children's cooking various parts of the meal. "The cousins" seem excited to cook their part of the meal, literally shooing me out of the kitchen while they prepare their dish for the "family feast."

Easter preparations may include recalling the joyous meaning of the holiday or participating in Lent. I have known people who celebrate Lent by sacrificial giving rather than giving something up. For instance, instead of giving up some treasured or desired object, they found a way, as a family, to give extra donations of time or money to those in need. Easter preparations also include special meals during Lent, Good Friday services, and any other special considerations you have prior to Easter.

As I mentioned earlier we enjoy making cookies as a family on the night before Easter as part of our preparatory rituals. The simple cookies are easy to make. Each ingredient and each step in the making of the cookie recalls some aspect of Jesus' crucifixion. The night ends as we put the cookies in the oven and seal it with tape (to mark the sealing of Jesus' burial tomb). In the morning we gather at the stove to find our cookies done—each one hollow and empty like Jesus' grave. We have a great time talking and sharing while we make the cookies. And at the same time we get to reinforce the message of Easter.

Each family may develop unique preparations that remind them of the true meaning of the holiday and bring the family together. During preparations, family members have the opportunity to celebrate one another and the values that ground their lives.

Of course, we all celebrate the "main event" of these rituals of tradition as well. On Christmas we share presents to honor the gift of Christ that God so generously gave us. On Thanksgiving we share a family meal, giving thanks for all the blessings from God. On Easter, we celebrate Christ's resurrection and then our new life in Him with a special family meal.

Rituals of tradition often carry an added challenge that everyday rituals do not. Specifically, we may celebrate at least part of the holiday with extended family. This can pose a challenge for many families. Will you celebrate with extended family? If so, how will you decide which family members to celebrate with? Which traditions will you attempt to carry into the extended family? Will you celebrate part of the holiday as a nuclear family and part with the extended family or will you celebrate the whole holiday with extended family?

Families have to determine how to enter into their individual ritual, transition into an extended family tradition, and then exit that extended family tradition. Although this can prove challenging, it is well worth the effort as your children get to experience the support and love of multiple generations as a part of the holiday ritual. A strong sense of family connection and continuity grows when multiple generations celebrate together. In addition, families can experience some different traditions and rituals. This presents an opportunity to evolve your family ritual and make it more meaningful and intimate.

Rituals Beyond the Family

Rituals often extend beyond the four walls of our home. For instance, family rituals can include friends as well as family. Perhaps your family has a family game night in which you invite another family or your children's friends to play games with you. We have a monthly game night at our church. Several families get together, share some food, and play games for about 3 hours one night each month. We begin the night with a meal, ice cream, or snacks. Then we play games. Finally, everyone helps clean up. It has become a great time that adults and children alike enjoy. And it is fun to watch the children begin to engage the adults in games and conversation.

When I was growing up, my family often went to another family's home on Friday night to play games. We had pizza and then the adults played cards while the children played games or watched a movie. This ritual made Fridays one of my favorite nights of the week.

Sometimes a family ritual may include various media. For instance, watching a movie or going to a concert together can become a family ritual. When our children were younger we had "mommy/daddy nights" in which my wife and I would stay up late watching movies with our daughters. One time I would stay up with one daughter and my wife with the other. The next time we would switch partners. To prepare for the night we would pick out movies together. Then we would make popcorn or get out the chips and pop. Finally, we would start the movies. Eventually we would all fall asleep. This ritual gave my wife and me time to spend laughing and talking with each daughter. It brought the media into our family ritual and afforded us the opportunity to talk about movies, indirectly teaching them discernment. It also provided an opportunity to teach our family values and beliefs in regard to the media. We did not do this in a lecturing way. Instead, we just laughed, enjoyed the movie, and talked.

Rituals that extend beyond the family may also include rituals around school or serving together in the community. One of the rituals we enjoy is serving together. We do this in simple ways at church by helping set up for game nights. We have also participated in one bigger ritual of serving together, going on a mission trip as a family. We had a wonderful time and, to this day, our children talk about their desire to return to the site of the mission trip.

Opportunities for rituals of connection and rituals of celebration abound. They are all around us. Take the time to think about the rituals that suit your own family. Enjoy putting the rituals into practice. As you do, you will find that the ritual helps you grow more intimate as a family. You will learn more about one another's daily lives, struggles, interests, hopes, and dreams. Family members will desire to spend time together as part of the ritual, even anticipating when the next ritual will occur. You will find yourself enjoying one another's company—all while having fun as a family!

18 FOR MARRIED ADULTS ONLY
....

"How beautiful and how delightful you are, my love, with all your charms! Your stature is like a palm tree, and your breasts are like its clusters. I said, 'I will climb the palm tree, I will take hold of its fruit stalks.' Oh, may your breasts be like clusters of the vine, and the fragrance of your breath like apples, and your mouth like the best wine!"

–Song of Solomon 7:6-9

"And as the bridegroom rejoices over the bride, so your God will rejoice over you."

–Isaiah 62:5

When I first entered Bible College I had a question. People looked at me like I was crazy when I asked them the question. But I genuinely wanted to know the answer. So I asked several of my friends, "Why does God not want us to have sex before marriage? Why wait?" When they gave simple answers such as "God created sexual intimacy for marriage," I would question further: "Why not make it OK to have sex once you are in love instead of married?" The answers usually ended up stating that God's command was for our benefit, i.e., to avoid the risk of pregnancy or STDs. But that did not satisfy me. *Did God create something as intimate, endearing, and apparently enjoyable as sex (I was not married at the time and did not know from firsthand experience) and then confine it to marriage simply because it protects us from unwanted pregnancy and disease?*

I still had this question in the back of my mind when I attended a church camp the following summer. The camp speaker spoke from 1 John 3:9 and noted how the "seed of God" abides in us and gives us power to resist sin. He told us that the Greek word for "seed" is *sperma*, a rather sexual term to a college-age male. Somehow the speaker's comment struck a nerve in me and a light came on. I began to catch a glimpse of God's intention for sexual intimacy. That glimpse continued to grow into a greater understanding of why God intends for intimate sexual relationships to occur only within the covenant boundaries of marriage. I began to see sex as more than just a physical act that might relieve sexual tension, satisfy physical desire, please another person, or even encourage an emotional connection and deeper love. I began to view sexual intimacy as a holy and sacred act, a beautiful metaphor of Christ's intimate connection with His Bride, the Church. Consider some of the aspects of this metaphor with me.

God is our Father and Jesus is our Bridegroom. The Church is the Bride of Christ. Jesus loves the Church and gave Himself up for her to present her without blemish or spot to His Father. She responds to His love with honor, respect, and submission. Within a covenantal relationship, the Bride grows deeper in love with the Bridegroom. She gains a deeper knowledge of her Bridegroom.

Jesus is the perfect Husband—faithful, honoring, loving, attentive, and sacrificial. His Bride, the Church, just loves to tell other people about His wonderful character. She shares His Word with others. The Seed of Christ (Holy Spirit poured out by Him) unites with the Word of God (also called the seed of God in 1 Peter 1:23 and Luke 8:11) to conceive a child of God. After conception, God's children remain in the protective womb of the Church to learn about God's family and to grow in maturity. They grow in their Father's image. After all, they have His seed or DNA, so to speak. Once mature, children leave the womb of the congregation with full knowledge that their Father (Jesus Christ) is always with them, "even to the ends of the world." If at any point God's children experience overwhelming hatred, stress, or temptation, they can run to the security of the Church (their mother) for encouragement, nurturance, comfort, and care. In this loving and nurturing environment, they are reminded that their Father (Jesus) has overcome the world.

A Sacred Union

God intended sex to create sacred and holy union. It unites two people, merging them into one flesh. As sewing one piece of cloth to another keeps the two pieces securely fastened and woven together, sexual intimacy weaves two people together. Sex becomes the ultimate bonding experience, the most physically pleasurable way to join two people together and create a sense of permanent attachment.

Sex provides a holy knowledge of the other person. The Old Testament speaks of sex as one person "knowing" another person. A man and woman are freed from inhibitions while in the presence of the one with whom they share sexually intimacy. They can fall into one another's arms and learn of one another's true essence. Sexual union presupposes an attentive and responsive love that seeks intimate oneness based on the deep knowledge of the one we love.

Sexual intimacy is a holy knowledge that results in the creation of new life. God alone is the Creator of all things. He has chosen, however, through the joining together of a man and a woman in sexual intimacy to bring new life into the world.

Sexual intimacy, then, is a holy ritual, a sacred metaphor of Christ's intimate oneness with His Bride, the Church. I no longer wonder why God wants us to wait until we enter a covenantal relationship (marriage) before engaging in sex. Our marital relationship, including making love, paints a vivid and beautiful picture of God's covenantal relationship with us, His Church. To enter that level of physical intimacy without the spiritual and emotional security of a covenantal relationship desecrates the true and complete unity of two physical, spiritual, and emotional beings.

On the other hand, I am no longer surprised that the devil attacks sex and twists it. He does not want anyone to recognize how this holy act proclaims the intimate, mysterious union of Christ to His Bride, the Church.

Within the covenant of marriage, sex becomes a sacred ritual that builds intimacy between a man and a woman, an intimacy as mysterious as the intimacy shared between Christ and His Church. The commitment, honor, grace, and forgiveness this covenant relationship provides make this intimacy both safe and secure. Sacrificially, partners desire to please one another above themselves and even begin to anticipate ways in which they might please one another. This anticipation and desire creates an even deeper sense of intimacy, honor, security, and safety.

This holy ritual leads each partner to express value for the other person and make efforts to discover new ways of satisfying the partner and making him feel loved. This, in turn, leads to greater pleasure for both partners.

Finally, this ritual leads to a growing identity of being one with your partner. Each partner no longer lives for self but for each other and for their relationship.

Let's Get Physical

Satan attacks sexuality with great fervor. He has spread vicious lies about sexual intimacy—lies that interfere with healthy relationships. One of

Satan's lies emphasizes the physical act of sex above the spiritual and relational aspects of sexual union. According to this lie, the physical pleasure and excitement "I" receive becomes the ultimate goal of sexual intimacy. Orgasm and the relief of sexual tension mark success. Anything short of orgasm is thus held to be incomplete, a failure.

Couples who focus on the physical aspects of their sexual relationship find that they cannot maintain the excitement. Focusing only on the physical aspects of sex leads to diminishing returns in pleasure. As a result, the couple may seek a variety of ways to maintain excitement in their sex life. This may lead to the use of pornography, affairs, or even "swinging"— opening the couple's sex life up to multiple partners. Even when the couple resorts to such props, however, pleasure and excitement slowly fade and the couple must seek something new and even more "edgy" to find the same level of fulfillment and excitement they once enjoyed by simply holding hands and gazing into one another's eyes.

The increased demand and expectation placed on sexual *performance* and the physical aspects of sex increases stress, and stress, in turn, can lead to a variety of sexual problems. Partners may feel used and objectified. Safety and security disappear. Trust diminishes. Each person feels a growing need to protect himself and focus on meeting his own sensual desires in the relationship. Ultimately, the couple who believes the lie that sex is all about physical pleasure becomes disillusioned, dissatisfied, and lonely.

Focusing on the physical aspects of sex will never produce ongoing fulfillment. Technique alone does not a happy marriage make. Only the sacred intimacy of spiritual and relational oneness can lead to ongoing pleasure, excitement, and fulfillment.

My Sexual Obligation

Another lie describes sex as a duty, an obligation to our spouse or to God. According to this lie, sex need not be enjoyable, only endured. I have heard two strains of this lie. Both sound spiritual but focus only on one aspect of God's overall picture of sexual intimacy. One strain recalls that God told Adam and Eve to "be fruitful and multiply" (Genesis 1:27). With this passage in mind, some say we must procreate. God commands it and we must fulfill our duty to God.

The second strain points to 1 Corinthians 7:2-5. In this passage, Paul tells husbands and wives to "stop depriving one another" and to "fulfill your duty" toward your spouse. Sex, then, becomes my duty to my spouse. I have to engage in sex with my spouse to fulfill my duty. Sex might become as mundane as taking out the trash or doing the laundry. My body belongs to my partner. I engage in sexual intimacy with my spouse out of obligation or demand that my partner engages in sexual intimacy with me due to their obligation.

Couples who believe this lie and focus only on the "obligation" and "duty" of sexual intimacy rob themselves of the true joy God intended married couples to experience. Treating sexual intimacy as mere duty does not communicate the love and oneness that God intends for couples to desire and experience. Without a deep, intimate expression of love, people begin to feel that their partner does not unconditionally love and value them. They start to feel anxious about their worth in their partner's eyes. Making love out of a sense of duty eventually becomes an anxious expression of need and a futile attempt to find validation of one's own worth. What appears on the surface as an obligatory act becomes a desperate attempt to elicit reassurance of value and love from one's partner.

Relationships based on these lies focus on "what I can get" rather than "what I can give." The anxious focus on "what I can get" arises from insecurity and fear. Honor is lost and partners, especially women, begin to feel objectified and used. Sex can then become a tool that one partner uses to make a point, withholds to express anger, or engages in to meet selfish needs and desires.

Both lies miss the mark of God's design for sexual intimacy within the covenant of marriage. Relationships that grow in the soil of these lies do not reflect God's intent for marriage. They do not reflect Christ's love for His Bride, the Church.

The Sacred Ritual by God's Design

God intends that married couples love one another and put one another's needs above their own, just as Christ did for His Church (Ephesians 5:25-27; Philippians 2:1-11). He intends for marriage to create an atmosphere of trust, safety, and security that will allow both partners to be completely vulnerable and open in relation to one another. In God's design for marriage, each partner grows increasingly secure in the knowledge that the other will love, protect, and provide for him. Spouses sacrificially give of themselves to make their partner more complete and whole. In other words, God designed the marriage relationship as a picture of His unselfish love for His Bride—a love so deep that He willingly gave up everything to lift Her up and provide Her an eternally secure relationship with Him.

God's intent for sexual relationships within the covenant of marriage builds on the foundation of, and desire for, emotional openness and mutual responsiveness. It results in fulfillment, satisfaction, and intimate connection. In fact, emotional connection leads to more satisfying physical connection, which, in turn, leads to more intense emotional connection. As this cycle continues, sexual relationships become more tender, playful, erotic, and exciting.

I teach a basic life development course to college students. During the discussion of early and middle adulthood, the question arises about who enjoys sex most, those with multiple partners or those in a long-term monogamous relationship. Students often think the person with multiple partners will find sex more enjoyable. The research suggests, however, that couples who have been happily married over time have the most enjoyable and satisfying sexual relationships (Berk, 2010). The love and commitment that hold a couple together over time build a sense of security that allows open expression, vulnerability, and a willingness to truly please one's partner. Short-term relationships, "hooking up," and "one-night stands" cannot produce the trust that provides a sense of security and safety. Only committed relationships in which the partners exhibit a willingness to listen to one another, prioritize one another's needs, and intentionally seek to please each other can produce the security that leads to the openness and vulnerability of truly satisfying sexual relationships.

The Sacred Ritual

The Scriptures speak of intimate relationship as a "cleaving" to one another. The Hebrew word used for "cleave" in Genesis 2:24 means to "cling to or stick to." The Greek word Jesus used in Matthew 19:5 and Paul used in Ephesians 5:31 when quoting Genesis 2:24 means "to glue to" or "to join one's self to another closely." In this sense, Scripture tells us that husbands are to glue themselves to their wives, to join to them closely.

When it comes to sexual intimacy, the Old Testament speaks of a man "knowing" his wife who then conceives (see Genesis 4:1). The Hebrew word for "know" (*yada*) means "to perceive by sight, touch, or mind" and "to know by experience." Sexual intimacy promotes a deep knowledge of our spouse, a knowledge based on the experience of all our senses that culminates in a mysterious and mindful awareness of the one we love.

This is not a book on sexual relationships, so I do not want to go into great detail on the act of sexual intimacy. I want only to stress that a couple's sexual relationship is a powerful ritual that brings intimacy to their relationship. Married couples who form an intentional Christian family will find a way to incorporate sexual intimacy into their lives. To do so, a couple must think about how to transition from the daily rush of life into the holy ritual of sexual intimacy.

Setting the Stage

As Kevin Leman (1999) says, "Sex really does begin in the kitchen." How we behave toward one another throughout the day sets the stage for a romantic interlude. Sexual intimacy occurs within the context of our whole life—work, house cleaning, parenting, spirituality, finances, and laundry.

Although this is true for both men and women, women appear particularly sensitive to the context of the sexual relationship. Experts tell us that a woman's sex drive results from a number of emotional factors including trust, closeness, feeling nurtured, gentle touch, the right words, and pleasant scents (Larimore, 2008). Even more, the actions and attitudes a woman's husband has displayed over the last day or even week can impact her feelings of romance and desire.

I often ask wives to help me explain this to their husbands. I begin by asking them what their husband has done in the past, or could do now, to increases her sexual desire for him. The husband generally sits dumbfounded as his wife describes actions such as running the sweeper, washing dishes, folding laundry, or playfully interacting with the children. We then discuss various commercials that exemplify this idea. (By the way, my personal favorite is the one in which a woman fantasizes about a man running the sweeper without his shirt on while saying, "That's the power of Lysol.")

All things considered, women need romancing to transition into sexual intimacy. Sorry to break the news to you, guys, but romancing her for half an hour will not cut the mustard. Romancing includes more than bringing home flowers, turning down the lights, and putting on soft music. These things are good, but true romance involves a lifestyle that expresses love for your wife. Honor her with your speech, your service around the house, and your awareness of her emotions, needs, and desires. Invest the time necessary to make your home a safe haven of trust and security, of unconditional love and acceptance.

This lifestyle will also require the husband to slow down the impulse to act on his sexual desire. I know that we men have strong desires that announce themselves at the drop of a hat and go from 0-60 in no time flat. But women need more time to "get in the mood." To honor your wife, slow down the desire to act. I did not say stop the desire but simply let it simmer rather than boil over. Attend to her emotional and physical needs as more important than your own. Let her recognize your love in your careful attention to her daily needs. It will all pay off in the end.

Women can set the stage for their husbands as well, but in a slightly different way. Men tend to be visually oriented. To transition into sexual desire they need only to see an attractive woman. So to help set the stage a wife can pay attention to how she looks. Put on something nice "just for your husband," something that allows him to see you and your beauty. After all, he will focus on you, not the candles and lighting in the room.

Some of you may be thinking, "But I'm not shaped the way I used to be." It is true—our bodies change with age. As intentional Christian couples, we need to offer our partners total and unconditional acceptance—physically, emotionally, and spiritually. This level of acceptance allows us to stand before one another naked and unashamed. Men, take the time to tell your wife about her beauty. Remember, we make beautiful what we love. When we express honor, value, and love for our wife, she will grow in beauty. If you have doubts about this, go back to chapter one and read it again.

Each person also needs to take care of the body God has given. I have heard many husbands tell me about their wife's beauty even when she minimized her beauty. Husbands often talk about their wife becoming more beautiful to them as she cares for her body. When we care for our body, we feel better. We perceive ourselves as healthier and more fit. We exude more confidence. We become more attractive.

Women can also take the time to "fix themselves up" for their husbands. Wear attractive clothing on various occasions and fix your hair up for your husband. By doing so you send a message to your husband that says, "I love you and value you enough to look attractive to you." Believe me, men find this very attractive.

Most importantly, cultivate your inner beauty. True outward beauty comes from within. It grows from a foundation of inner beauty and character (1 Peter 3:2-3). One psychologist, Rand Hassen, conducted an experiment that supports inward beauty (www.youtrubo.com/Article/ShowArticles.asp?ArticleID=299). He showed several subjects a picture of the same person and asked them to rate that person's attractiveness. Half the subjects received the picture associated with descriptions of "mean-hearted character" traits whereas the other half received the same picture associated with descriptions of "kind-hearted character" traits. Those who associated the pictured person with "kind-hearted character" traits reported him as more attractive than those who associated the pictured person with "mean-hearted character" traits. This study suggests that a person's character impacts how others perceive him or her. Others perceive those with positive character as more attractive than their counterparts with negative character.

My uncle first showed me a stain-glassed window in his church at nighttime. They were pretty. When I returned in the daytime, however, and saw the sun shine through the stain glass the pretty picture became breathtaking. True beauty is seen only when the light of strong inner character shines through. It is not something physical. We may not be a "perfect 10" by worldly standards, but inner beauty causes a person to exceed the "perfect 10" in the eyes of our spouse.

The Sacred Union

Together, the couple has set the stage by honoring one another, attending to one another's needs, and focusing on one another's unique interests. In the process they have created a safe and romantic atmosphere of intimacy and mutual admiration. The actual physical act of sexual intimacy represents a culmination of this growing sense of intimacy and admiration that began with mutual honor and grace.

Communication remains an important component of sexual intimacy. Even during the physical act of sexual intimacy, a couple communicates love and affection through gentle touch and loving words. They communicate acceptance and mutual pleasure as they hold one another. As a husband intentionally focuses on his wife and strives to please her, he validates her importance and communicates her level of priority in his life, and vice versa.

As the couple enjoys one another's love, they can verbally note any touch or action that is especially pleasurable. Each person can also gently ask the partner to stop any touch or action that is uncomfortable or not pleasurable.

When your partner tells you something is pleasurable or asks you to stop doing something that is uncomfortable, listen! They are allowing you to know them better, teaching you how to deepen your intimacy with them and express your love for them. Take pleasure in the knowledge that your partner feels secure enough in your arms to share such intimate details. Treat that information with precious, tender care because it allows you to grow more intimately and deeply entwined as a couple. Through this communication, you create a deeper sense of oneness.

Savor the Moment

All good things must come to an end, but do not let this sacred moment slip away too quickly. Sexual intimacy leads to relaxation, a melding into one another's arms. Men experience a release of oxytocin after sexual intimacy. This chemical helps build a stronger emotional bond to the wife with whom he has become sexually intimate. It also brings them more in touch with their feminine, softer side (Larimore, 2008). As a result, the moments after sexual intimacy often provide an opportunity to talk on a deeper, emotional level. Share statements of love, attraction, and affection. Take time to rest in one another's arms and enjoy the moment of deep intimacy and union. Hold one another and share. Deepen your relationship before rolling over to go to sleep or jumping into the day's activities. Rest and relax in one another's presence.

Conclusion

In *Kosher Sex* (1999), the author states that "sex is humankind's loftiest pursuit, where a man and a woman, freed from all inhibition, can capture the other's essence." Perhaps true sexual intimacy comes the closest to returning us, if only for a moment, to that time in which sin had not enticed man, a time in which husband and wife stood before one another and God naked and unashamed, each seeking to care for and serve the other. Sexual intimacy bonds us together in a mysterious union that God designed at the beginning of time, a union that portrays Christ's love for His Bride, the Church. Sexual intimacy is a sacred gift from God. Unwrap that gift with honor and grace so you can celebrate with the intimacy, joy, and fervor God intended.

CONCLUSION

. . . .

"'You shall love the Lord your God with all your heart, and with all your soul, and with all your mind.' This is the great and foremost commandment. The second is like it, 'You shall love your neighbor as yourself." On these two commandments depend the whole Law and Prophets."

—Jesus, Matthew 22:37-40

"For the whole Law is fulfilled in one word, in the statement, 'You shall love your neighbor as yourself.'"

–Paul, Galatians 5:14

I find families fascinating. They constantly change. About the time I figure out how to practice honor and grace while celebrating my family, I get a curve ball. You know what I mean. Just when I think I have figured out how to celebrate marriage with my wife, sharing honor and grace on a daily basis, one of several curve balls suddenly comes our way—one of us changes work schedules, the water heater breaks and we are broke, we move to a new house and the plumbing unexpectedly blows, or we have a child. Suddenly everything I thought I knew becomes a swing and a miss. I have to start reassessing and learning all over again.

I was living in honor, grace, and celebration with my wife when we had our first child. We were thrilled to have a child. But with her came a sudden lack of sleep, changing schedules, new sounds and noises, a huge increase in work load, changing diapers, cleaning up after exploding diapers, constant monitoring.... We were exhausted and irritable. Suddenly, treating my wife and child with honor and grace became much more challenging.

I tried to get up before the baby in order to start my day with some quiet time. Our daughter, on the other hand, had an uncanny sense of when I rolled out of bed. No matter how early I got up, she would begin to cry and not stop until I held her. Suddenly, my time was not my own. My life was not my own. My schedule was not my own.

In the midst of this exhaustion, honor, grace, and celebration became more challenging to live out. How do I show honor, grace, and celebration to a newborn who only cries, eats, gazes, poops, and sleeps? How do I show honor, grace, and celebration to my wife when she is exhausted, irritable, and hungry, just like me? I had to turn to God to learn more honor, grace, and celebration. Perhaps that is part of God's intent for our lives—that we constantly turn to Him for help in meeting the challenges of life.

Don't get me wrong. I would not trade parenthood for anything. I love having children. Having children is one of the most exciting, rewarding, and satisfying aspects of life. Having children taught me to better love my wife. Children also increased (and continue to increase) my understanding of how to live a life of honor and grace. I would not have near the celebration in my life if not for the joy that my wife and my children bring into my life as well as the lessons of innocent and abandoned celebration I learn from my children.

I only mention the challenges because they point out the fact that families constantly change. Every time I think I have a handle on it, I swing at a curve ball and miss. I fall short of my goal to live out God's honor, grace, and celebration in my family. Celebrations turn into irritations when a family member is exhausted from work or life. Simple misunderstandings suddenly become frustrating arguments that escalate into WW III rather than opportunities to show honor. We apologize, yes, but the grace of forgiveness is hard to come by at times. Children still learning how to get along begin arguing for the umpteenth time about who gets to sit on that one spot on the couch and I blow my stack. The curve ball got me swinging at air again. I begin to get discouraged. Will I ever get this "family thing" right? Can I ever show honor, grace, and celebration on a consistent basis?

One day when I was feeling discouraged a proverb came to mind— "Love covers all transgressions" (Proverbs 10:12)—followed by a similar statement—"Love covers a multitude of sins" (1 Peter 4:8). Perhaps the most important aspect of forming a strong family flows from love. When bathed in love, family member can overlook mistakes and episodes of falling short. Love covers offenses. Family members continue to love in spite of weaknesses and shortcomings. In fact, we could sum up the whole of this book by saying that God's design for families centers on love.

Love Honors

Honor flows out of love. When we love someone we seek to become a person of honor in her eyes. We behave in a way that will elicit respect and adoration from her. Rather than arrogance, we exhibit humility. Rather than seeking to have our own desires met, we seek to meet the desires of the one we love. Loving families honor others with kindness and strive to do things that will benefit them. Family members search out opportunities to show kindness in their deeds and words, to be useful and helpful to one another. Love leads family members to treat one another respectfully and strive to know more about one another so they can please and show kindness to each other.

When families practice love, they believe the best about one another. They believe that each person wants the best for the family and has good intentions and pure motives. Family members entrust themselves to one another because they believe each family member will hold that trust with integrity. When the other person says or does something hurtful in a moment of anger, family members who love one another look beyond the words to the emotions underlying the words. They maintain a hopeful belief that the other person truly loves them and simply did not know how hurtful the comment was or did not mean it the way it came out. In families of love the members believe the best about one another. Rather than accuse one another of meanness, they let their love put the best possible face on an action and always believe the best.

Love Shows Grace

Grace also flows out of love. When family members love, they remain patient with one another in the midst of disagreements or arguments. Rather than lash out with anger and revenge, loving people forgive. They do not respond to provocations with resentment or vengeance but with kindness and patience. In loving hope, they wait to see what impact loving patience will have on the other person's behavior. When they confront the negative behavior, they do so with honor and grace, gently and lovingly.

Those who love do not hold grudges. They are not jealous or suspicious but believe the best about one another's intentions and actions. Instead of hurting and opening up old wounds, loving families cover them and allow them to heal. When they disagree they do not pick at old wounds to inflict the most pain but instead focus only on the issue at hand, allowing the old wound to rest and heal. They forgive those who have hurt them and seek reconciliation, not revenge.

When family members focus on their love for one another, they do not publish the faults of others or keep a running tally of good and evil words and deeds. They do not expose one another's shortcomings and bring that person to greater shame. Instead, family members address any shortcomings and faults privately rather than publicly. Quietly, families of love practice gentle, loving correction with the hope and expectation of reconciliation.

Love Celebrates

Celebration also flows out of love. Families of love celebrate the truth. They rejoice and celebrate when other family members grow in godly character and practice integrity, generosity, compassion, and love. When celebration flows from love, family members rejoice in fairness and seek to show justice in their actions toward one another. Loving families celebrate innocence and mutual trust. They celebrate the opportunities to show honor to one another by giving preference to one another's needs and desires without concern for equity and repayment.

Loving families experience freedom from fear. After all, "perfect love casts out fear" (1 John 4:18). Instead of fear, loving families experience safety, security, and peace. They are free to celebrate with abandon because they have perfect security, knowing that they have the unconditional acceptance of their family. Even when punishment becomes necessary, family members know that it is done for their own good and that they remain an integral and loved member of the family.

Loving families have great hope for one another. They hope for the best for each and every family member. As a result, they rejoice in one another's successes and accomplishments without jealousy or insecurity. They celebrate each family member's unique contributions with no fear that their own success will get "lost in the shuffle." Loving families realize that another person's success does not detract from any other person's success. All are equally important, valued, and celebrated. In fact, families of love look at one another as more important than themselves, not looking out for their own personal interests but also for the interests of others (Philippians 2:3-4). As a result, each member of a loving family can wholeheartedly celebrate each person's success.

The Qualities of Love

You might recognize those qualities above. They are qualities of honor, grace, and celebration. They are qualities of love. Many weddings include a reading of these qualities in a familiar verse form. Let me finish with that verse:

"Love is patient, love is kind and is not jealous;
Love does not brag and is not arrogant,
Does not act unbecomingly;
It does not seek its own, is not provoked,
Does not take into account a wrong suffered,
Does not rejoice in unrighteousness, but rejoices with the truth;
Bears all things, believes all things,
Hopes all things, endures all things.
Love never fails…
But now faith, hope, and love, abide these three;
But the greatest of these is love." (1 Corinthians 13:4-13)

I pray that your family will become a celebrating community of honor and grace, a family of love.

APPENDIX

Development

Dobson, J. (2001). *Bringing up boys: Practical advice and encouragement for those shaping the next generation of men.* Tyndale.

Gurian, M. (2002).*The wonder of girls: Understanding the hidden nature of our daughters.* New York, NY: Pocket Books.

McMinn, L.G. (2000). *Growing strong daughters: Encouraging girls to become all they're meant to be.* Grand Rapids, MI: Baker Books.

Nelsen, J., Erwin, C., Duffy, R. (1995). *Positive discipline for preschoolers: for their early years-raising children who are responsible, respectful and resourceful.* Rocklin, CA: Prima Publishing.

Newton, R.P. (2008). *The attachment connection: Parenting a secure & confident child using the science of attachment theory.* Oakland, CA: New Harbinger Publications, Inc.

Sears, W., Sears, M. (1995). *The discipline book: Everything you need to know to have a better behaved child-from birth to age ten.* New York, NY: Little, Brown, & Company.

Birth Order

Leman, K. (1999). *Sex begins in the kitchen.* Grand Rapids, MI: Baker Book House Company.

Leman, K. (1998). *The birth order book: Why you are the way you are.* Grand Rapids, MI: Revell.

Love Language

Chapman, G. (2007). *The heart of the five love languages.* Chicago, IL: Northfield Publishing.

Chapman, G., Campbell, R. (1997). *The five love languages of children.* Chapman & Campbell.

Smalley, G., Trent, J.T. (1993). *The blessing.* Nashville, TN: Thomas Nelson, Inc.

Personality

Feldhahn, S. (2004). *For women only: What you need to know about the inner lives of men.* Colorado Springs, CO: Multnomah Publishers.

Feldhahn, S., Feldhahn, J. (2006). *For men only: A straightforward guide to the inner lives of women.* Colorado Springs, CO: Multnomah Publishers.

Smalley, G. (1996). *Making love last forever.* Dallas, TX: Word Publishing.

Tieger, P.D., Barron-Tieger, B. (2001). *Do what you are: Discover the perfect career for you through the secrets of personality type (3rd edition).* New York, NY: Little, Brown & Company.

Temperament

Nelsen, J., Erwin, C., Duffy, R. (1995). *Positive discipline for preschoolers: for their early years-raising children who are responsible, respectful and resourceful.* Rocklin, CA: Prima Publishing.

Sears, W., Sears, M. (1995). *The discipline book: Everything you need to know to have a better behaved child-from birth to age ten.* New York, NY: Little, Brown, & Company.

OTHER RESOURCES: JOIN THE HONOR GRACE & CELEBRATE COMMUNITY

The *Honor, Grace, Celebrate* website (www.honorgracecelebrate.com) offer resources to enhance your ability to follow God's design for your family. On this website you will find several beneficial resources including:

- A weekly blog dealing with various issues related to family, marriage, or parenting.

- A list of other resources available for family issues. In addition, you will find several of the resources reviewed.

- A description of the Family Bank of Honor. This section includes a listing of over 40 ways to show honor and grace to family members as well as ways to celebrate family.

Join *Honor, Grace, Celebrate* on Facebook. The Facebook page offers daily ideas including: Honor Hints, Gifts of Grace, and Celebrate. You will also find daily links to various articles related to family issues.

BIBLIOGRAPHY

Barna Research Group. (2008). New marriage and divorce statistics released.http://www.barna.org/FlexPage.aspx?Page=BarnaUpdate&BarnaUpdateID=295. 3/31/08: obtained January 16, 2009.

Bolt, M. (2004). Pursuing human strengths: A positive psychology guide. New York, NY: Worth Publishers.

Bonhoeffer, D. (1995). The cost of discipleship. New York, NY: Touchstone.

Boteach, Schmuley. (1999). Kosher Sex. New York, NY: Random House.

Bronson, P., Merryman, A. (2009). Nurture shock: New thinking about children. New York, NY: Grand Central Publishing.

Brown, S. (2009). Play: How it shapes the brain, opens the imagination, and invigorates the soul. New York, NY: Avery.

Cherlin, A.J. (2009). The marriage-go-round: The state of marriage and the family in America today. New York, NY: Alfred Knopf.

Christenson, L. (1970). The Christian family. Minneapolis, MN: Bethany Fellowship.

Chapman, G. (2007). The heart of the five love languages. Chicago, IL: Northfield Publishing.

Chapman, G., &Campbell, R. (1997).The five love languages of children. Chapman & Campbell.

Covey, S.R. (1989).The 7 habits of highly effective people: Powerful lessons in personal change. New York, NY: Fireside.

Davis, D.E., Hook, J.N., &Worthington, E.L. (2008). Relational spirituality and forgiveness: The roles of attachment to God, religious coping, and viewing the transgression as a desecration. Journal of Psychology and Christianity, (27) 4, 293-301.

Dobson, J. (2001). Bringing up boys: Practical advice and encouragement for those shaping the next generation of men.Carol Stream, IL: Tyndale.

Doherty, W. (1997).The intentional family: How to build family ties in our modern world. New York, NY: Perseus Books.

Doherty, W. Overscheduled kids, underconnected families: the research evidence. http://www.puttingfamilyfirst.org/research.php. Obtained January 16, 2009.

Duda, K. (Ed) (2003). The American family. New York, NY: H.W. Wilson Company.

Elkind, D. (1981). The hurried child: Growing up too fast too soon. Reading, MA: Addison-Wesley..

Feldhahn, S. (2004).For women only: What you need to know about the inner lives of men. Sisters, OR: Multnomah Publishers.

Feldhahn, S., &Feldhahn, J. (2006). For men only: A straightforward guide to the inner lives of women. Sisters, OR: Multnomah Publishers.

Gardner, T.A. (2002). Sacred sex: A spiritual celebration of oneness in marriage. Colorado Springs, CO: Waterbrook Press.

Goleman, D. (1995). Emotional intelligence: Why it can mater more than IQ. New York, NY: Bantam Books.

Gottman, J. (1994). Why marriages succeed or fail. New York, NY: Fireside.

Gottman, J.M., & Declaire, J. (1997).Raising an emotionally intelligent child: The heart of parenting. New York, NY: Fireside.

Gottman, J.M., & DeClaire, J. (2001).The relationship cure: A 5 step guide to strengthening your marriage, family, and friendships. New York, NY: Three Rivers Press.

Gottman, J.M., &Silver, N. (1999).The seven principles for making marriage work: A practical guide from the country's foremost relationship expert. New York, NY: Three Rivers Press.

Gurian, M. (2002).The wonder of girls: Understanding the hidden nature of our daughters. New York, NY: Pocket Books.

Gurian, M. (1996).The wonder of boys: What parents, mentors and educators can do to shape boys into exceptional men. New York, NY: Tarcher/Putnam.

Hall, J.H., & Fincham, F.D. (2008).The temporal course of self-forgiveness. Journal of Social and Clinical Psychology, (27) 2, 174-202.

Hass, A. (1994). The gift of fatherhood: How men's lives are transformed by their children. New York: NY: Fireside.

Hellinger, B., Weber, G., &Beaumont, H. (1998).Love's hidden symmetry: What makes love work in relationships. Phoenix, AZ: Zeig, Tucker, &Co.

Jacob, C.L. (2000). Eat the fat, drink the sweet, and be merry: A biblical defense for play on the Lord's Day. IIIM Magazine, Online, (2) 1, March 20-26, 2000.

Johnson, S. (2008). Hold me tight: Seven conversations for a lifetime of love. New York, NY: Little, Brown &Company.

Kendrick, S., &Kendrick, A. (2008).The love dare. Nashville, TN: B & H Publishing Group.

Kimmel, T. (2004).Graced based parenting. Nashville, TN: Word Publishing Group.

Kohn, A. (2005). Unconditional parenting: Moving from rewards and punishment to love and reason. New York, NY: Atria Books.

Kroeger, C.C. (2005). Toward a more comprehensive understanding of wifely submission.Christian Counseling Today, 13 (3), 38-42.

Larimore, W., &Larimore, B. (2008).His brain, her brain: How divinely designed differences can strengthen your marriage. Grand Rapids, MI: Zondervan.

Leman, K. (1999). Sex begins in the kitchen. Grand Rapids, MI: Baker.

Leman, K. (1998). The birth order book: Why you are the way you are. Grand Rapids, MI: Revell.

Maio, G.R., Thomas, G., Carnelley, K.B., &Fincham, F.D. (2008). Unraveling the role of forgiveness in family relationships.Journal of Personality and Social Psychology, (94) 2, 307-319.

Markman, H., Stanley, S., & Blumberg, S.L. (1994). Fighting for your marriage: Positive steps for preventing divorce and preserving a lasting love. San Francisco, CA: Jossey-Bass, Inc.

Mayo Clinic Staff. (2007). Forgiveness: How to let go of grudges and bitterness. http://www.mayoclinic.com/health/forgiveness/MH00131, Obtained October 20, 2009.

McDowell, J. (2000). The disconnected generation: Saving our youth from self-destruction. Nashville, TN: Word Publishing.

McMinn, L.G. (2000). Growing strong daughters: Encouraging girls to become all they're meant to be. Grand Rapids, MI: Baker.

McMinn, M.R., Thompson, R.D., Fervida, H., Trihub, B.L., Louwerse, K.A., Pop, J.L., & McLeod-Harrison, S. (2008). Forgiveness and Prayer.Journal of Psychology and Christianity, (27) 2, 101-109.

Medhus, E. (2001) Raising children who think for themselves. New York, NY: MJF Books.

Narramore, B. (1980). Adolescence is not an illness. Old Tappan, NJ: Fleming H. Revell.

Nelsen, J., Erwin, C., &Duffy, R. (1995).Positive discipline for preschoolers: for their early years-raising children who are responsible, respectful and resourceful. Rocklin, CA: Prima Publishing.

Newton, R.P. (2008). The attachment connection: Parenting a secure & confident child using the science of attachment theory. Oakland, CA: New Harbinger Publications.

Packer, J.I. (1973).Knowing God. Downers Grove, IL: Intervarsity Press.

Scalise, T. (2008).Generational Patterns and strongholds.Christian Counseling Today, 16 (1), 24-26.

Sears, W., &Sears, M. (1995).The discipline book: Everything you need to know to have a better behaved child-from birth to age ten. New York, NY: Little, Brown, & Company.

Seligman, M.E.P. (2002). Authentic Happiness: Using the new positive psychology to realize your potential for lasting fulfillment. New York, NY: The Free Press.

Seligman, M.E.P., Reivich, K., Jaycox, L., & Gillham, J. (1995).The optimistic child: A proven program to safeguard children against depression and build life long resilience. New York, NY: Harper Collins Publishers.

Smalley, G. (1996). Making love last forever. Dallas, TX: Word Publishing.

Smalley, G., & Trent, J.T. (1993).The blessing. Nashville, TN: Thomas Nelson.

Spring, J.A. (1996).After the affair: healing the pain and rebuilding trust when a partner has been unfaithful. New York, NY: Harper Collins Publishers.

Spurgeon, C. (2000). Grace and Power. New Kensington, PA: Whitaker House.

Stratton, S.P., Dean, J.B., Nonneman, A.J., Bode, R.A., &Worthington, E.L. (2008). Forgiveness intervetions as spritiual development strategies: Compairing forgiveness workshop training, expressive writing about forgiveness, and restested controls. Journal of Psychology and Christianity, (27) 4, 347-357.

Tieger, P.D., &Barron-Tieger, B. (2001). Do what you are: Discover the perfect career for you through the secrets of personality type (3rd edition). New York, NY: Little, Brown & Company.

Toff, B. (2008). Survivor wins for CBS. Nytimes.com. October 4, 2008: obtained January 16, 2009.

Thomas, G.L. (2004). Sacred parenting: how raising children shapes our souls. Grand Rapids, MI: Zondervan.

Thomas, G. L. (2000). Sacred Marriage: What if God designed marriage to make us holy more than to make us happy? Grand Rapids, MI: Zondervan.

Wade, N.G., Worthington, E.L., & Haake, S. (2009). Comparison of explicit forgiveness interventions with an alternative treatment: A randomized clinical trial. Journal of Counseling and Development, (87) Spring 2009, 143-151.

Waite, L.J., & Gallagher, M. (2000).The case for marriage: Why married people are happier, healthier, and better off financially. New York, NY: Broadway Books.

Witherspoon Institute (2006). Marriage and the public good: Ten principles. Princeton, NJ: The Witherspoon Institute.

Worthington, E.L., Hook, J.N., Davis, D.E., Gartner, A.L., & Jennings, D.J. (2009). Reach: An evidence-based group intervention to help Christians forgive. Christian counseling Connection, (16) 4, 9-10.

Worthington, E.L. (2001). Five steps to forgiveness: The art and science of forgiving. New York, NY: Crown House.

www.whatisgrace.org/sermonnotes/2008/0210_parenting6_faith.pdf. Downloaded June 1, 2010.

Yancey, P. (1997). What's so amazing about grace? Grand Rapids, MI: Zondervan.

CPSIA information can be obtained at www.ICGtesting.com
Printed in the USA
267521BV00002B/1/P